Tangled in Terror

'I am profoundly grateful to Suhaiymah Manzoor-Khan for writing this book. It is brave. It is necessary. It is true. It is what we Muslims have been waiting for. A brilliant, powerful and moving account of Islamophobia, not as an individual moral deficiency, but as rooted in colonial histories of white supremacy and global capitalism. For me, *Tangled in Terror* triggered long-felt pain, anger, grief at the abuse, torture and genocidal violence Muslims are made to suffer the world over. Violence which not only evades accountability, but seems at times not even to register as harm. Manzoor-Khan carefully traces the origins and shape of the historical and ongoing terrorisation of Muslims, revealing untold injustices, and showing us how to untangle ourselves from terror and instead find threads of resistance.'
—Nadine El-Enany, author of *(B)ordering Britain* and
Co-Director of the Centre for Research on Race and Law

'Courageously makes explicit the implicit unfreedoms of our society.'
—Lowkey, poet and rapper

'An unflinching account of the forces that have converged to cast Muslims as a permanent threat while profiting off our marginalisation.'
—Aamer Rahman, writer and comedian

'Lyrical and uncompromising – Suhaiymah writes to disrupt.'
—*gal-dem*

'A fearless writer who cuts through nonsense. Suhaiymah's voice is one of the most exciting of her generation.'
—Fatima Manji, award-winning broadcaster, *Channel 4 News*

'This is the first time the breadth and depth of the Islamophobia we face has been collated in one place and analysed with such precision. It really feels like "our" book.'
—Moazzam Begg, author of *Enemy Combatant: The Terrifying True Story of a Briton in Guantánamo* and outreach director for CAGE

'Suhaiymah's writing is fierce and clarifying. She understands that the task is to resist oversimplified definitions of Islamophobia and instead turn the reader's attention toward its political function – how it increases proximity to violence and impoverishes us all.'
—Lola Olufemi, author of *Feminism, Interrupted*

Outspoken by Pluto
Series Editor: Neda Tehrani

Platforming underrepresented voices; intervening in important political issues; revealing powerful histories and giving voice to our experiences; Outspoken by Pluto is a book series unlike any other. Unravelling debates on feminism and class, work and borders, unions and climate justice, this series has the answers to the questions you're asking. These are books that dissent.

Also available:

Mask Off
Masculinity Redefined
JJ Bola

Border Nation
A Story of Migration
Leah Cowan

Behind Closed Doors
Sex Education Transformed
Natalie Fiennes

Lost in Work
Escaping Capitalism
Amelia Horgan

Make Bosses Pay
Why We Need Unions
Eve Livingston

Feminism, Interrupted
Disrupting Power
Lola Olufemi

Burnt
Fighting for Climate Justice
Chris Saltmarsh

Split
Class Divides Uncovered
Ben Tippet

Tangled in Terror

Uprooting Islamophobia

Suhaiymah Manzoor-Khan

First published 2022 by Pluto Press
New Wing, Somerset House, Strand, London WC2R 1LA

www.plutobooks.com

British Library Cataloguing in Publication Data
A catalogue record for this book is available from the British Library

ISBN 978 0 7453 4541 3   Paperback
ISBN 978 0 7453 4545 1   PDF
ISBN 978 0 7453 4543 7   EPUB

This book is printed on paper suitable for recycling and made from
fully managed and sustained forest sources. Logging, pulping and
manufacturing processes are expected to conform to the environmental standards of the country of origin.

Typeset by Stanford DTP Services, Northampton, England

Simultaneously printed in the United Kingdom and United States of
America

Contents

Acknowledgements

More thanks than I can mention are owed for this book. In honesty, it is the culmination of thinking I have been doing for most of my adult life and therefore a product of conversations and lessons learned from so many people, books, lectures, passing comments, poems, calls, late-night conversations, khutbahs, voice-notes and everything in between.

But I want to take some space in particular to thank Azeezat. Thank you for helping me to hear myself, for being honest with me, and for pushing me to write the version of this book that mattered most to me. Your care and generous capacity for imagining and listening have shaped so much of what I hope this book can be. And thank you for also reminding me that I am allowed (and hope) to change and grow after this.

Special thanks also go to Phelan, for always being beside me in the discursive trenches and having my back in untangling every set of ideas we stumble upon. To Bava, for making me feel unconditionally supported, for sharing a persistent hopefulness in the face of despair, and for reminding me that truths are more multifaceted than we like to admit. To Alaa, for teaching me how to listen to and value the unglamourous dreams and forms of resistance that surround us; and for your encouragement which comforted me at some of the most difficult parts of writing this.

I would also like to thank everybody who took time to read chunks of drafts of this book and asked me questions that made me think harder and dive deeper – thank you, Tarek, Sita,

ACKNOWLEDGEMENTS

Maryam, Lily, Shereen, Azfar and Muneeza. Huge thanks also go to the people whose voices weave in and out of this book – Hajera, Latifa, Rizwaan, Faima, Imam Shakeel, Suhraiya, Fahad, Nadine, Sumaya, the team at HHUGS, and Moazzam, thank you for giving me your time, truth and often your vulnerability. Thanks also go to those whose influence is equally present in this book, though they go unnamed. In particular, all the children who in poetry workshops, classrooms, mosques and after-school clubs, have taught and reminded me that not only is another world necessary, it is always already being imagined, and so incredibly worth it.

Thank you Neda, for trusting me to do this, for all your care, and for enabling me to write without bending to parameters that felt looming. I am so grateful for the ways you have seen what I have tried to do.

This book would simply not exist without my family's love, support and faith in me. No words can suffice. To Mummy, Saif, Sumaiyyah, Nani and Nana, thank you for your patience, for keeping me alive through the isolation of writing in a pandemic, for your unconditional love, and for seeing and believing in me even when I don't. It is you who show me what love makes possible.

Above all else, the praise and thanks are ultimately to Allah, whom I owe every single thing to and whom I pray accepts this book and its intentions.

Introduction: Not what it is but what it does

The standard narrative about Islamophobia goes like this: Islamophobia is an unfair bias against Muslims that exists because of right-wing media sensationalism, the rise of the far-right, and Brexit voters. Their rhetoric leads to hateful verbal and physical attacks against Muslims. Therefore, the solution to Islamophobia is more legal consequences to deal with Islamophobic 'hate-crimes', more positive representation of Muslims in the media, more work to challenge stereotypes, and more Muslims in positions of decision-making. As a result, there are continuous debates about defining Islamophobia and running inquiries into its presence within political parties and Parliament. In this narrative, 'the Islamophobes' are people like Donald Trump, Katie Hopkins, Tommy Robinson, Nigel Farage, and at a push, Boris Johnson.

But this version of Islamophobia is reductive. It has no history or context. Islamophobia does not exist because of the lack of laws against it, or the lack of Muslim MPs and peers. Nor does it exist because people do not know enough about Muslim contributions to the nation, or because Muslims have not spent enough time proving 'what Islam really says'. Instead, Islamophobia persists despite these things, precisely because such solutions keep the conversation about Islamophobia away from addressing its root historical and structural causes.

In this book, I present a very different picture of Islamophobia. It is the outcome of colonial histories of white supremacist racial hierarchy and global capitalism that have generated a story about Muslims as threats, barbarians and misogynists. That story is used by governments and industries across the world today to garner popular consent for projects that violate and destroy people's lives. Because, in the name of 'security' against 'the Muslim threat', liberal populations consent to types of dehumanising and illiberal treatment that they would never accept for themselves. From illegal invasions to indefinite imprisonment and deportation, to the indignity of everyday surveillance and destruction of life and property. These projects are not random, they have financial and ideological advantages for those who benefit from a deliberately exploitative world order.

In other words, Islamophobia is not 'the new racism', nor has it existed since ancient times. It is one strategy of a colonial world-system that was built over a period of 500 or more years. Far from broken or ended, the operation of Islamophobia today proves that this system is still at work. It functions through processes of imperialist occupation, theft of resources and dislocation of people; procedures of coercive and brutal policing and caging; and measures of co-option, social-engineering and ideological control. We must depart from thinking about Islamophobia as an individual moral deficiency. It is an outcome of historical developments that now ripen the conditions required for mass expulsion and genocide of both the gratuitous, spectacular kind, but also the corrosive, almost invisible kind.

Islamophobia is not a problem for Muslims alone, and cannot be tackled on its own. It is not a single-issue struggle but a problem for the world, related to all racisms, all forms of oppression, border violence, policing, war, environmental catastrophe, gender-based violence and injustice. The standard narrative about Islamophobia hides that it is less about Muslims than it is about everything else. Therefore, this is not a book about

Muslims or Islam. This book is not interested in proving whether Islamophobia exists to those who do not have to face its violence every day, or in piling 'explanation on explanation to name the violence'.[1] Nor is it interested in how we should specifically define Islamophobia. Instead, this book asks what Islamophobia *does*. And how understanding its function is central to understanding how we can build a world that is safe for all oppressed, exploited and marginalised people, rather than a world that is 'secure' for nation-states to repress, and imperialist capitalist interests to accumulate profit. The only way Islamophobia can be uprooted is by sowing the seeds for another world altogether.

Not about Muslims

While Islamophobia is not *about* Muslims, and certainly not only about Britain, it is useful to recognise some components of the Muslim population here, as this is where my analysis primarily focuses. Official records and popular representation often refer to us as being solely from Pakistani and Bangladeshi heritages. But such imaginings erase the significant proportion of Muslims in Britain from Somali, Nigerian, Afghan, Iraqi, Moroccan, Turkish and Caribbean heritages,[2] as well as Muslims from a range of other backgrounds encompassing every continent and race. I am therefore conscious that my positioning as a Muslim of Pakistani heritage leaves me open to blind spots, and particularly to erasure of the intersection of anti-Black and Islamophobic manifestations of white supremacy that Black Muslims experience the sharp end of. I have tried to counter-

---

1 Sahar Ghumkhor, *The Political Psychology of the Veil: The Impossible Body* (Palgrave Macmillan, 2020), p. ix.

2 Rokhsana Fiaz and Laurence Hopkins, Understanding Muslim Ethnic Communities – Summary Report (London: DCLG, 2009).

act such erasure in the pages that follow since we cannot uproot Islamophobia without uprooting all manifestations of racism, but I cannot claim to have overcome my positionality altogether. This is important to bear in mind as we move forward in our interrogation and to not lose sight of as we work for another world.

Alongside Britain's Muslims being mainly Black and brown and therefore facing the well-known institutional racism and deprivation that comes with this, Muslims also 'experience the greatest economic disadvantages of any group in UK society'.[3] 50% live in poverty – the highest proportion of any religious group.[4] Well-established correlations tell us that poverty impacts every other aspect of a person's life from mental health to nutrition, and quality of schooling to housing and even quality of air. As the COVID-19 pandemic has reinforced, race and poverty directly impact people's risk of physical ill-health and death. Consequently, it is unsurprising that Muslims had the highest rate of COVID-19-related deaths compared to other religious and non-religious groups in England throughout the first year of the pandemic.[5] Considering this, it is extraordinary that those on the political Left routinely exclude and marginalise Muslims from their concerns. There can be no meaningful struggle to transform relations of economic exploitation unless Muslims' experiences are understood as structurally shaped by the racially distinct impact of capitalist relations as a consequence of Islamophobia. This is a theme I come back to throughout the book.

3 Social Mobility Commission, The Social Mobility Challenges Faced by Young Muslims, (London: SMC, 2017), p. 1.

4 The Muslim Council of Britain, British Muslims in Numbers, (London: MCB, 2015), p. 46.

5 Office for National Statistics, Deaths involving COVID-19 by religious group, England: 24 January 2020 to 28 February 2021 (London: ONS, 2021).

Moreover, while Muslims made up around 5% of the UK population in the last census,[6] we make up over 15% of the prison population.[7] With so many Muslims in Britain locked behind bars, or locked into cycles of poverty, the structural nature of Islamophobia is clear. Muslims also make up 50% of those detained in UK immigration removal centres like Brook House.[8] This serves as a reminder that Muslims are disproportionately displaced across the world by the impacts of imperialism past and present that devastate lives, economies and environments through war, resource depletion and enforced debt. Any work that aims to support refugees or tackle climate change should therefore have intimate knowledge of Islamophobia. Especially because Islamophobic anti-immigrant rhetoric is often precisely what is used to distract us from recognising the origins of displacement and environmental catastrophe in the first place.

Understanding Islamophobia's root causes therefore helps connect resistance to it, with multiple and international struggles.

Writing to transform our realities

Given this, I have written this book to aid us in building a world that is just, and not only liveable, but safe for everyone. I regularly work with school children who are so accustomed to depictions of themselves as terrorists, threats, barbarians, misogynists and foreigners, that the poems they write in our workshops are riddled with such images and words. I ask myself

---

6   MCB, Muslims in Numbers.

7   Raheel Mohammed & Lauren Nickolls, *Time to end the silence: The experience of Muslims in the prison system* (London: Maslaha, 2020).

8   Brook House Independent Monitoring Board, Annual Report (London: HMP, 2013), p. 12.

what it would take to change the world of their poems. What would their poems look like if they had the language to name the oppression they face, as opposed to only naming themselves through it, or in opposition to it? And what would their poems look like if they lived in a world where they felt safe? These questions matter because those children matter.

The most successful means of ending oppression is to empower those who are oppressed. Consequently, I am not interested in writing a book that reproduces academic debates about Islamophobia or in contributing to conversations about defining it; I am interested in how analysing our social realities can help us transform them. I therefore write without steering away from my Muslimness or holding it at arms-length. I refuse to be the Muslim author often desired by middle-class pundits. Instead, I believe Allah is the source of truth and creation and I believe my primary purpose is to worship Allah. This makes it incumbent on me to strive for the sake of Allah to expose injustices, speak truth to power and resist oppression. I pray that intention guides my writing and this book in total.

If my Islam is an obstacle to being taken seriously by a reader, or a cause for an eye-roll or raised eyebrow, it is worth considering how that reader is already invested in characterising Muslims as unintelligent and embarrassingly unmodern. It is also worth considering what parameters such a reader would require me to write within to be considered 'objective' enough for the violence of Islamophobia to be valid. As I explore later, secularism is too often assumed as an inherently objective way of viewing the world, and religion as its inverse. But secularism is born from a specific history and is entangled in the project of constructing European white supremacy. Consequently, secular does not mean neutral. It is the concept that invents the category of 'religion' and gives it meaning in the first place. If we are too invested in it to see that, we are invested in the same project of Eurocentric domination that underpins Islamophobia itself.

As much as this book is focused on Islamophobia as part of a set of global power dynamics, I also want to centre the fact that Islamophobia lives under the skins of those of us who it marks. Islamophobia alters our physiologies through trauma, lives in our nervous systems, makes us hypervigilant and afraid. I cannot write this book 'outside' of Islamophobia because I live within it. If I write pretending that Islamophobia has not been present in the ways I have written, the choices I have made, and the concerns I have had about how it may *sound*, and how it could *look*, I would be pretending Islamophobia is simply the topic of this book. But when I finish writing this book, as much as I may be done with Islamophobia, it will not be done with me.

This book might make you uncomfortable, but if you stick with me perhaps you will come to see that a reductive understanding of Islamophobia as just an experience of hate or prejudice at the hands of Islamophobes is not just misguided, it deliberately diverts us from seeing the violence of the world and thus produces solutions that pose no challenge to it. This prevents us from seriously understanding the reasons that over 1 million Muslims are in concentration camps in China's Xingang province, being burned alive in the streets of Delhi, persecuted and forced to leave their homes in Myanmar, drowning in boats off the coast of Greece and Italy, trekking for thousands of miles across the Sahara desert from Mali, Chad and Niger, fleeing drone strikes in Somalia, sitting in refugee camps in Syria, revolting for their lives to matter against the police state in the USA, unable to access their natural resources in Palestine, and being policed, imprisoned, detained and monitored in the UK and across Europe.

Beyond explaining what Islamophobia is, let us ask the much more important question of what it does, and what *we* are doing about it.

Chapter 1

A history of race-making: Inventing 'the Muslim threat'

After the police murders of George Floyd and Breonna Taylor in the summer of 2020, and the subsequent Black Lives Matter uprisings across the world, institutions from body cosmetic companies to universities issued public solidarity statements. These often talked of tackling racism more urgently by no longer tolerating it. Such declarations symbolised the prevalence of the idea that racism is something institutions choose to tolerate, or not tolerate, and therefore that it is an outside force brought in by 'bad apple' individuals, rather than something already engrained within the normal working of things. This assumption leads many to believe that racism can be resolved through individualistic approaches such as increased awareness of unconscious biases, or by acknowledging our privileges.[1] But these solutions allow institutions, organisations and governments to proclaim themselves anti-racist without addressing how systematic exclusion, exploitation and oppression based on race are central and foundational to their working. This is not the result of ignorance, or a mistake; it is a convenient and reductive reframing of the racism at hand.

---

1   Azfar Shafi & Ilyas Nagdee, *Recovering Antiracism, Reflections on collectivity and solidarity in antiracist organising* (Amsterdam: Transnational Institute, 2020).

8

Individualising racism makes it almost impossible to discuss it as a system of power related to capitalism and colonialism. Instead, in the mainstream, racism is usually only acknowledged when it manifests in physical attacks or explicit verbal abuse – as the virality of countless graphic videos shows us. But racism is rarely acknowledged when it manifests in more regular ongoing violence such as intergenerational poverty, systematic exclusion from adequate healthcare and housing, and methodical exploitation of labour.

One consequence of this is that when I say that 'Islamophobia is a form of racism', people think only of so-called Islamophobic 'hate crimes', which are by no means insignificant, but more a symptom than a cause of Islamophobia. The other consequence is that people claim Islamophobia cannot be a form of racism because Muslims are a religious grouping, not a race. But what is 'a race'? Clarifying this question is central to any anti-racism efforts, and there can be no meaningful uprooting of Islamophobia without engaging with the history of racism in the first place.

Common sense tells us that racism exists because different races exist. But the opposite is in fact more accurate: races were invented to facilitate and justify racism. There is no natural set of races that existed prior to people devising them. In fact, a central part of the project of European colonialism was the invention of races. Since colonialism was a process of dominating and subjugating to exploit and profit from the resources and labour of colonised lands and people, colonisers classified those people and places as naturally inferior races.[2] This masked theft, dispossession and genocide.

---

2 For more on colonialism see Frantz Fanon, *The Wretched of the Earth* (New York: Grove Press, 1963); Edward Said, *Orientalism* (New York: Pantheon Books, 1978); Walter Rodney, *How Europe Underdeveloped Africa* (London: Bogle-L'overture Publications, 1972).

For example, in the 1830s the American physician, Samuel Morton, conducted measurements of human skulls to justify colonialism and slavery as somehow 'natural' due to the skulls of some 'races' being smaller than others.[3] This was a project to not only classify distinct races as having distinct levels of intelligence or strength, but to place them in a hierarchy with white Europeans at the top. Rather than a product of nature, we must consequently understand racial categories as ideological tools developed to reinforce and justify racism, which was a part of justifying colonialism more broadly.

Enlightened racism and imagined Otherness

Like Morton, others also used scientific enquiry to mask their creation of racial hierarchy as neutral and objective projects. This was particularly common during the so-called Enlightenment period in Europe – in and around the 1700s – which is important to note because in popular discourse this era is celebrated as one in which progressive ideas of human rights and universal freedom were invented. We rarely speak about the fact that those ideas were formed within what was also the golden age of colonial white supremacy and capitalism; and that that means from their very inception, liberal ideals of freedom never extended to include enslaved and colonised people. In fact, much of the work to conceptualise race was undertaken to justify not extending those ideals to everyone.[4]

Racial hierarchy was theorised by many famous Enlightenment thinkers who are still widely loved today. For example,

3   https://sciencedaily.com/releases/2018/10/181004143943.htm   (accessed   July 2021).

4   https://slate.com/news-and-politics/2018/06/taking-the-enlightenment-seriously-requires-talking-about-race.html (accessed July 2021).

David Hume wrote, 'There never was a civilized nation of any other complexion than white . . . No ingenious, manufactures among them, no arts, no sciences . . .'[5] By asserting this, Hume not only constructed a racial hierarchy linked to intellectual and cultural superiority; he attributed an inherent lack of value to people without 'white complexion'.

Similarly, Immanuel Kant asserted that 'Humanity is at its greatest perfection in the race of the whites', attributing increasingly less value to 'yellow Indians' and other sub-categories of his own making. He also claimed all societies must therefore follow the same trajectory as Europe to advance.[6] This theory of development is one we see frequently used in international aid and development projects today which continue to assign non-Europeans with not only inferior value, but as occupying an alternative time altogether: stuck in a past of primitiveness, lawlessness and religious superstition, while white Europeans are modern, constitutional and enlightened.

Many other thinkers from the Enlightenment period could be quoted to demonstrate the way racial hierarchy was invented. But what is crucial to recognise in these projects of race-making is that the various classifications of humanity created 'whiteness' as much as any other race. Whiteness was not constructed as simply a skin colour, instead, to this day it is an ideology of power, a mark attributed to valued lives and knowledge, and a context from which European theories of equality and freedom emerged. White European supremacy is therefore baked into ideas we hold as universal common sense, not something unique to Hitler and neo-Nazis. Far from it, in fact, white supremacy is the historical inheritance of European liberal democracies, and

---

5 David Hume, *Essays and Treatises on Several Subjects Vol. IV* (London: A. Miller, 1768).

6 Ed. Emmanuel Chukwudi Eze, *Race and the Enlightenment: A Reader* (Oxford: Blackwell, 1997), pp. 38–64.

can be seen everywhere today from NGO work, to news media, to the assumptions that underpin law, policy, childcare, borders and more.

It is important to recognise that writers advancing notions of racial hierarchy were not part of an overarching conspiracy to invent racism, though. Instead, as Edward Said famously theorised in *Orientalism*, whether intentional or not, the way Europeans represented racial 'Others' through reports, letters, novels, travel journals, paintings, map-making, economic texts or anything else, produced a body of knowledge – a discourse – which actually said less about the lands and people they were supposedly about, than they did about how Europeans imagined themselves. Indeed, Said suggested their representations were more about defining 'the West' as the inverse of whatever 'the East' was, and for this reason, he referred to their project as constructing 'the Other'.[7]

The writings of one of Britain's foremost colonisers, Lord Cromer, exemplify this. In Westminster Abbey, central London, a white marble memorial reads, 'To the glory of God and in memory of Evelyn Baring 1st Earl of Cromer 1841–1916. Regenerator of Egypt.' Referring to him in this way suggests that Cromer saved Egypt from degeneration. However, as colonial administrator of the Egyptian treasury, he reduced the capacity of Egyptian textile factories by refusing to protect them against British imports of Egyptian cotton that was spun in the UK then sold back to Egypt. Far from regenerating Egypt, these actions deindustrialised it and extracted all value from its economy to Britain.[8] Cromer also underfunded Egypt's education system and

---

7   Said, *Orientalism*.

8   http://asma-lamrabet.com/articles/muslim-women-s-veil-or-hijab-between-a-colonial-ideology-and-a-traditionalist-islamic-ideology-a-decolonial-vision/ (accessed February 2021).

flogged, imprisoned and put to death those who resisted him. On top of this, in Britain itself Cromer was a strong opponent of women's suffrage – in fact he was the first president of the National League for Opposing Women's Suffrage.

Considering this, it is ironic that Cromer wrote, 'women's status in Egypt as well as in all the Mohammadian countries hinders their development and advancement to be amongst the civilised nations.'[9] His statement declared a disingenuous concern for 'women's status' in Muslim countries to justify colonial oppression that actively worsened economic and educational conditions for women. Cromer also wrote that Egyptian women's veils, rather than British subjugation, were a 'fatal obstacle' to Egypt becoming 'civilised'.[10] Such tropes and tactics will be familiar to readers because anxieties about Muslim women's rights and dress are still used by those who have no serious concern about women's well-being, to justify and conceal the violence of military occupations, policing and other oppressions that this book explores. Likewise, Muslims are still depicted by academics, journalists and governments as Others who do gender 'wrong' – whether through Muslim men being perceived as violent patriarchs, paedophiles or sexually frustrated 'terrorists'; or through Muslim women being imagined as their victims, or deceptive and alluring accomplices. All these characterisations are rooted in the colonial imagination where, just as Said argued, claiming that racial Others were underdeveloped was actually about establishing Britain as 'advanced'; and declaring 'Mohammadians' as misogynistic was a way of claiming Europeans were stalwarts of equal rights.

---

9   Ibid.
10   https://theguardian.com/world/2002/sep/21/gender.usa (accessed November 2020).

Clearly, constructing and attributing racial categories with different civilisational, intellectual, physical and human value was always political, and has been the work of centuries. No single theorist or coloniser produced racial hierarchy and it is important to note that their representations of colonised people and places were inconsistent, contradictory and sometimes even challenged at inception. Nonetheless, racial hierarchy has been a central ideological tool used by Europeans to facilitate geopolitical and economic projects of enslavement, exploitation and oppression. In this book I therefore use the terms 'Europe', 'West' and 'Western' not to suggest they are tangible or static entities, but to refer to them as constructs themselves that are the result of long histories of violence and dispossession.

Intolerant secularism

Most conversations about racism today overlook the way that secularism was also constructed as a part of white European supremacy. This is crucial to understand and linked to another key shift during the Enlightenment period: the idea that truth stemmed no longer from God, but from European men. Rene Descartes's famous philosophical statement, 'I think, therefore I am', symbolised this. Being (I am), was no longer a result of God's creation, but man's own rationality (I think). The 'I' of the statement was not imagined as universal, though. As Nelson Maldanado-Torres argues, in the context of colonialism and racial hierarchy, the concept implied, 'I think (others do not think, or do not think properly), therefore I am (others are not, lack being, should not exist or are dispensable)'.[11] In simpler terms, as Yassir Morsi writes, it meant 'I am white, therefore I

11 Nelson Maldonado-Torres, 'On the Coloniality of Being', *Cultural Studies*, Vol. 21, 2007, pp. 240–70, p. 252.

14

think' – a statement about racial Others being unable to think or hold knowledge.[12]

This was symbolic of a wider shift in which humanity would now be judged not by God, but by closeness to the ideal of the enlightened European, who would himself be the judge of it – able to replace God's standpoint and neutrality over all beings. Enlightenment Europe's claim to leave belief in God 'behind' in this way was crucial. It meant that classifying Others as religious, was just another method of designating their underdevelopment compared to Europe. The construction of racial inferiority has always been connected to how we understand and judge the category of 'religion' then.

This is better understood by looking at the history of secularism as an idea. Far from the claim that it is a condition of living free from the influence of religion, secularism invented the category of 'religion' and what counts as religious life.[13] It emerged as a European political project over a period when states were trying to limit the institutional power of the Church so they could enforce their own authority. They did not do this by destroying Christianity, but by declaring it should be confined to 'personal conviction' and therefore limited to the level of private conscience or 'the home'.

But at the same time, Europe was using Christianity to secure geopolitical interests – most European states sent and supported missionaries overseas to gain footholds for invasion and domination.[14] Such activity was widespread by the mid-1800s, well after Europe was claiming to be too rational for religion.

---

12   Yassir Morsi, *Radical Skin, Moderate Masks: De-radicalisation and Racism in Post-Racial Societies* (London: Rowman & Littlefield, 2017), p. 61.

13   Saba Mahmood, *Religious Difference in a Secular Age: A Minority Report* (Princeton University Press, 2015), p. 33.

14   Ibid., p. 34.

Clearly, secularism was never about ensuring neutral public space, it was a tool used contradictorily to limit the power of the Church over European states, and to advance their interests.

As the late scholar Saba Mahmood wrote, this contradiction generated the paradoxical situation where, by the 1950s, 'as international law became secular in its language, rationale and stipulations, it also came to root itself in Europe's unique Christian heritage'. That heritage was imagined to be superior in morals, humanity and modernity 'especially when measured against the barbarity of Islam'.[15] It is obvious here that religion was never imagined separately from race or as the inverse of 'secular' either. Instead, Europe was imagined as superior due to *both* its Christianity *and* secularism. This inconsistency is illustrated in more of Cromer's writings. He claimed that Christianity in 'the East' had 'stagnated' because its followers were 'Orientals' and thus it 'has been surrounded by associations antagonistic to progress'.[16] Here, we see that religion was not inherently deemed a mark of backwardness, however, when practiced by racial Others (Orientals), even Christianity could mutate into the 'stagnant' phenomenon of 'religion'.

When I run workshops exploring Islamophobia with young Muslims, the stereotypes they most frequently mention are the ways they're assumed to be unintelligent, irrational and unmodern. They are interpersonally and institutionally belittled based on these perceptions which are directly traceable to colonial theories that constructed their beliefs and knowledge as tainted by their supposed racial backwardness. And this is not only limited to their Islam. Think of the way the education system teaches European thought as universally relevant 'philosophy', but ideas from elsewhere as area-specific, 'African

---

15 Ibid.
16 Ibid., p. 44.

religion', 'Eastern medicine', or 'Oriental thought'.[17] A specific set of ideas from a relatively small region of the world at a very precise time (Enlightenment Europe) cannot be considered the only legitimate way for everyone everywhere to think about truth, knowledge, or ourselves. Far from ensuring toleration, as young Muslims tell me all the time, the bias and intolerance of such a worldview is constant. And as scholar and researcher Suhraiya Jivraj told me, 'we're still very much bound by the idea of civilising our populations to be "secular moderns"'.

Racialising religion

The contradictions in the discourses relating to secularism are explored further in Chapter 7, but an important point to mention here while we consider the history of race-making, is that contemporary Europe's religious heritage is not even solely Christian, or 'Judeo-Christian' as is sometimes claimed. For 700 years, between the eighth and fifteenth centuries, much of Spain and Portugal was ruled by Muslims whose intellectual impact created the conditions for Europe's Renaissance.[18] The Muslims of that area (the Iberian Peninsula) were known as 'Moors'. These were initially a group of indigenous North Africans and Arabs, however, by the time the Islamic dynasty fell in 1492, most Moors in the peninsula were descendants of Iberian converts.[19] By that time they were indispensable to the social fabric and economy of the peninsula, nonetheless, the new Catholic

---

17   Dipesh Chakrabarty, *Provincializing Europe* (Princeton University Press, 2000), p. 30.

18   https://blackhistorymonth.org.uk/article/section/history-of-slavery/africa-before-transatlantic-enslavement/ (accessed July 2021).

19   Richard Fletcher, *Moorish Spain* (New York: H Holt, 1992).

rulers forced them, along with Jewish people, to convert to Christianity or be expelled.

Historians estimate that around a million Moors were deported and expelled from the region over the next 200 years.[20] Those who stayed and converted faced suspicion over their loyalty to Catholicism which was blurred with fears that they may support an Ottoman invasion. This eventually led to the belief that their old religion was actually in their blood, preventing them from becoming true Christians. Christians of Moorish heritage were subsequently discriminated against in certain professions, university colleges, and so forth. Here, we should notice that a blurred distinction developed between what we might today call a 'religious group', and hereditary characteristics we often call 'race'. Religion had almost 'racial' dimensions as early as the 1500s.

As Catholic Spain began colonisation of the Americas, these ideas about impure blood trickled into debates about indigenous Americans too. Could they be converted to Christianity or would their old religion remain in their blood like Moors? Did they even have souls to be converted? These discussions about whether indigenous people were the same species as Europeans fed into decisions about how they would be treated. A soulless population could be murdered without Catholic Spain worrying about whether its actions were 'just' – they weren't human after all.[21]

As masses of indigenous Americans were killed through genocide and the spread of European diseases, colonisers looked elsewhere for a free labour force to exploit the resources of the

---

20 Matthew Carr, *Blood and Faith: The Purging of Muslim Spain, 1492–1614* (London: Hurst & Company, 2017).

21 Mandalado-Torres, *Coloniality of Being*, p. 246.

land. Sub-Saharan Africans were deemed the ideal choice.[22] Unlike indigenous Americans, there was no debate about whether they were the same species as Europeans. It was conveniently decided that they were naturally suited for slavery and their humanity was stripped and commodified for European profit. Yet even here, enslaved Muslims were imagined distinctly from their non-Muslim counterparts due to conceptions of Moors. This further reveals the entanglement of what we consider race and religion.

For instance, in 1522, after enslaved Muslims from West Africa led the first recorded slave revolt in Hispaniola Island (today's Haiti and Dominican Republic), Charles V of Spain attempted to exclude 'slaves suspected of Islamic learnings' from the Americas.[23] Much of his concern about enslaved Muslims being especially likely to revolt was linked to previous anxieties about the Moors as treacherous. Such historical connections remind us that the USA's current imagining of its Black and Muslim populations as 'dangerous' has entwined roots in the colonial imagination since the first Muslim presence in the Americas was African. This history helps exemplify both why anti-Muslim racism cannot be toppled without also toppling anti-Black racism; and why claims that Muslims are outsiders to the West are fabricated.

Historical classification of groups of people as threatening, soulless or impure are part of the same system geared at enabling the political and economic ambitions of the West that today classifies us as dangerous, religious and fanatical.

---

22   Ibid., p. 247.
23   https://medium.com/s/story/the-misidentification-of-black-muslims-2de4d 214da12 (accessed, September 2020).

Islamophobia cannot end while white supremacy survives

My point is not that visible differences between us don't exist. They do. But when looking even very briefly at race and racism as historical inventions, we see that those differences have not always carried the meanings they do now. Historic prejudices or oppression that existed between people who looked different – such as pre-colonial forms of colourism – did not impose meanings about how human, civilised or intelligent people were based on comparison to European whiteness as the standard. This is what distinguishes ideas of racial difference as we know them today. They are inseparable from the project of European colonialism and Eurocentricity. Therefore the centrality of race and racism to our lives and world is a stark reminder that colonialism is not merely a wrong that occurred in the past, it is ongoing and infused into the fabric of our world.

Wealth made from owning racialised people – people categorised into races – their resources, or lands, is the basis of institutions and dynamics around us today from welfare systems to banks, universities, and corporations. Conversely, theft of those resources that ravaged and polluted lands is the reason millions of people are displaced and seeking asylum in Europe today. Colonialism's impact also survives in terms of the ideas we accept as common sense and those we reject; the ways we think about knowledge, geography, economy, governance and ourselves; our aspirations, criteria for judging value and truth, and the ways we categorise behaviours and space itself. Some scholars call this lasting impact, 'coloniality'.[24] In Nelson Maldanado-Torres's words, although colonialism may be over in

---

24   Maldonado-Torres, *Coloniality of Being*.

many visible ways, 'as modern subjects, we breathe coloniality all the time and every day'.[25] It is only through understanding the omnipresence of this that we can begin to understand Islamophobia as but another manifestation of racism.

'Race' comes from historical contexts, not nature. A Moor in thirteenth-century Europe might be racialised as 'African-American' in 1980s New York, or 'Muslim' in London today. The races we categorise ourselves and each other into are informed by a broad history and evolve according to contemporary political circumstances. In the words of the late cultural theorist and activist, Stuart Hall, race is a 'signifier'. That means that even with 'the biological, physiological or genetic definition [of race], having been shown out the front door', race 'tends to sidle around the veranda and climb back in through the window'.[26] In other words, although experiments like Morton's skull measuring have lost popularity over time, we still try to root explanations for 'social, political or cultural phenomena' within the 'racial character' of people.

The most obvious example when it comes to Islamophobia is the way that 'terrorist violence' is explained as the outcome of something innate in Muslims: their racial character. In other words, instead of seeking out the root causes of such violence, we are told it is the outcome of Muslim 'culture', 'religion' or 'ideology'. Even those who say terrorism is only the problem of a minority of Muslims, concede that it *is* a Muslim problem. In this way, culture, religion, and ideology all rearticulate race because they are imagined as internal essences Muslims carry within us, which clash with 'Western' values/culture. And much as Orientalists and Enlightenment thinkers described physical

---

25   Ibid., p. 243.
26   Stuart Hall, *Race, The Floating Signifier* transcript, (Online: Mediaed, 1997), p. 7.

features, geography or women's dress as signs of racial inferiority, today think tanks, psychologists, academics, intelligence agencies, police, criminologists and governments describe hijabs, beards, speaking Arabic, eating halal food and more as signs of the 'Muslim essence' of violence, irrationality and barbarism. This is the construction of race, and because Muslims are brutalised, policed, exploited and made disposable based on being racialised in this way; this is racism.

Additionally, people who are not Muslim but are assumed to be based on how they look or act, also face violence because of this racialisation. For example, turban-wearing Sikh men have been attacked for being assumed to be Muslim. And, notoriously, Jean Charles da Silva e de Menezes, a Brazilian man, was murdered by London Met Police in 2005 after they profiled him as one of the 7/7 bombers due to what they called his 'Mongolian eyes'.[27]

Racial oppression is not based on the 'truth' of race then, it is an ideological strategy that dehumanises whole groups of people for tangible material – usually financial – benefit. Therefore, we cannot end Islamophobia without eradicating coloniality in its entirety. Overwhelming as that may seem, it *can* be eradicated in its entirety because things have *not* always been this way. Anything that has a historical beginning can also have an end, but anti-bias training, positive representation and access to positions of power won't cut it. We must instead commit to completely ending our investment in coloniality which means, as abolitionist Mariame Kaba puts it, 'we ourselves will also need to transform . . . [because] we are deeply entangled in the very systems we are organizing to change'.[28]

---

27 https://theguardian.com/commentisfree/2015/nov/18/shoot-to-kill-terror-fear-prejudice-jean-charles-de-menezes (accessed December 2020).
28 Mariame Kaba, *We Do This 'til We Free Us: Abolitionist Organizing and Transforming Justice* (Chicago: Haymarket Books, 2021), p. 4.

For many people of colour that means we will need to stop seeking proximity to whiteness that involves participating in racial hierarchy at the expense of our Black siblings. And for all of us it means not only opposing the impacts of coloniality when they manifest as ugly and sensational oppression, but also when they manifest as liberal, secular values. Such values – inclusion, toleration or 'privatisation of religion' – are the vocabulary of coloniality, and therefore of exploitation and extermination. As we will explore, this is clear in the ways those values are often evoked to mask racist projects and strategies. They enable denial and erasure of the racism of colonial states like Britain today by asserting that the West cannot be the home of racism because it is the home of rationality, secularism and rights. But such liberal values 'at home' were always sustained by oppression 'over there'.

Chapter 2

Never-ending pillaging in the name of international security

When we saw my husband's body, we had no choice but to drop everything and run. We fled for our lives. Even left our cattle behind . . . our homes destroyed, livestock destroyed, crops destroyed, people obliterated. And now we don't even have a single bag, let alone a home to go to . . . When it rains the children and I take shelter under a tree. – Hawa Haji Aden, Janale, Somalia.[1]

Mustafa, how can I describe him? He was my first child. He made my life beautiful. He was nearly two years old . . . The call for evening prayer began and everyone was indoors, breaking fast. The next thing I know, Mustafa is next to me with his guts in the dirt. I realised my arm was cut open and the flesh was stripped away from my hip . . . The doctor said he couldn't operate on Mustafa and we should prepare to say goodbye . . . The wound in my heart will never heal. – Nidhal Abed, Fallujah, Iraq.[2]

1   https://bylinetimes.com/2020/05/06/so-much-agony-and-suffering-eye-witness-accounts-of-us-somalia-drone-strikes/ (accessed Jan 2021).
2   https://bbc.co.uk/iplayer/episode/p08kr4ws/once-upon-a-time-in-iraq-series-1-3-fallujah (accessed August 2020).

They stripped the brothers naked, they sliced off their clothes with a knife, they shaved our beards until I saw brothers who had beards – older brothers with white beards – crying like babies . . . After this they took us onto this aeroplane and soldiers armed with M16s and Glock pistols pushed us into the bowing position. Chains on our legs. Chains on our hands. Hoods on our heads . . . dogs barking, guns clicking, pointed at us . . . Are they going to kill me? Am I going to see my family again? . . . Are they now just a memory in my head? – Moazzam Begg, Birmingham, England.[3]

No number of voices would be sufficient to capture the incalculable destruction, misery and death of the so-called War on Terror. Its bombings, raids, drones, torture, abduction, rape, displacement, abuse and extermination will shape generations to come. But for some, the War on Terror sounds like a relic of the past – something to do with 9/11, George Bush, Afghanistan and Iraq. But with 'our boys' largely home, and bogeymen like Osama bin Laden dead, we hardly seem to be at war anymore. Yes, ISIS still exist, and we hear about drone strikes now and then, but the world goes on, right?

On the contrary, the War on Terror has become constant and borderless in the name of promoting international security against a seemingly ever-growing terrorist threat. This threat, whom the USA openly declared war against in 2001, now appears to exist everywhere from a wedding in Afghanistan, to train carriages in Madrid, a mall in Nairobi, to a café in the southern Philippines, a concert in Manchester, and a funeral in Nigeria. Everywhere is apparently embroiled in the *same* war with the same 'terrorist enemy'. But who has been made safer by

---

3   https://youtube.com/watch?v=Uyn5uqdIP2A (accessed September 2020).

this securitisation of the world? And what does focus on 'the terrorist threat' hide?

Whose terror? Whose war?

The narrative of the War on Terror assumes that the world is split between good, freedom-loving people and terrorists. This racialised distinction is built through the colonial imagination as well as more recent orientalist theories by the likes of Bernard Lewis and Samuel Huntington. In the 1990s they claimed there was a fundamental culture clash between 'the Muslim world' and 'Western civilisation', that would shape the twenty-first century.[4] Just ten days after 9/11, US President George Bush tapped into this in his famous declaration, 'Our war on terror begins with al-Qaeda, but it does not end there . . . Every nation, in every region, now has a decision to make. Either you are with us, or you are with the terrorists.' It appeared as if 9/11 had split the world in two, which, in US Secretary of State, John Ashcroft's words, it did, 'September 11 drew a bright line of demarcation between the civil and the savage'.[5]

These reductive colonial distinctions of the civil West and savage East are given life every time we use the language of 'terrorism' and 'terrorists'. Such words undermine our understanding of the causes of violence because they depoliticise them. Whether 'the terrorist' is called an Islamist, jihadi, enemy combatant, suicide bomber, fundamentalist or extremist, the cause of their violence is said to be Muslim culture, ideology or religion – a racial essence. These explanations mean that terrorism is understood as a threat inherently bound up with Muslim

---

4   Bernard Lewis, 'The Roots of Muslim Rage', *The Atlantic*, 1990.

5   Richard Jackson, *Writing the War on Terrorism* (Manchester University Press, 2005), p. 62.

existence. This logic is eventually genocidal since it means the cause of terrorism is not a political issue to be resolved; it is Muslimness which can only be resolved through elimination.

However, there is another way to understand 9/11 beyond taking Muslimness as the *explanation* for violence. Those responsible for 9/11 – generally believed to be Osama bin Laden and al-Qaeda – were originally born from guerrilla groups of insurgents that the US government and CIA exploited, funded, armed and trained during the 1970s and 1980s. The US did this in an attempt to contain communist influence after the Soviet Union invaded Afghanistan in 1979. But after the Soviets withdrew, the US lost interest in the region, creating a power vacuum in which civil war erupted, embroiling factions of the CIA-trained guerrillas. In the 1990s organised groups born from those origins began using the methods taught by the CIA to respond to imperialist US foreign policy.

For example, in 1993, in retaliation to US diplomatic support of Israeli state violence against Palestinians, there was an attempt to blow up the World Trade Centre traced to formulas 'taught in CIA manuals'.[6] Records show that US intelligence experts had anticipated such a response and were unsurprised by it. In fact, in 1998 when US Embassies in Nairobi, Kenya and Dar es Salaam, Tanzania, were bombed in response to other US foreign policy, suspects included Osama bin Laden, and the US Secretary of State predicted 'every likelihood that there will be a further large bomb and other kinds of attack.'[7]

In that context, 9/11 is not the 'day that changed everything', caused by people who are exceptionally violent. It is part of a

---

6 Noam Chomsky, *Hegemony or Survival: America's Quest for Global Dominance* (London: Penguin, 2004).

7 https://web.archive.org/web/20000530211831/http:/www.state.gov/www/regions/africa/board_introduction.html (accessed October 2020).

political pattern of violent responses to US foreign policy. In fact, bin Laden, who claimed he masterminded 9/11, wrote that the motivation was 'very simple: because you attacked us and you continue to attack us', referring to US violence in Somalia, collaboration with the Israeli state against Palestinians, and the Indian state against Kashmir.[8] He explained, 'Your forces occupy our countries, you spread your military bases throughout them, you corrupt our lands, and you besiege our sanctities'. Considering this, 9/11 can be better understood as a manifestation of a type of political violence used by many non-state groups against imperialist powers throughout the twentieth century.[9] In fact, 'Muslim terrorist attacks' in the West over the past two decades have been repeatedly explained by their perpetrators as motivated by Western foreign policy. Even Western intelligence and military leaders concede that this is the primary cause of such violence.[10]

The language of 'terrorism' therefore hides the root causes of violence by focusing on a cultural/religious explanation. A genuine concern about violence would instead lead to ending imperialist foreign policy that terrorises people across the globe, and that is the initial violence 'terrorism' responds to. In scholar Arun Kundnani's words, 'violence in the "war on terror" is relational: the individuals who become ISIS volunteers are willing to use violence; so too are our own governments. We like to think our violence is rational, reactive and normal, whereas theirs is

---

8   https://theguardian.com/world/2002/nov/24/theobserver (accessed August 2020).

9   https://opendemocracy.net/en/violence-comes-home-interview-with-arun-kundnani/ (accessed March 2021).

10   Arun Kundnani, *The Muslims Are Coming! Islamophobia, Extremism and the Domestic War on Terror* (Oxford: Blackwells, 2014).

fanatical, aggressive and exceptional. But we also bomb journalists, children and hospitals.'[11]

Moreover, it is worth asking which kinds of violence do *not* terrorise? For example, gender-based violence in Western immigration detention centres and prisons, at the hands of policemen and guards, not only harm their immediate victims but send a message to other women to consequently live in fear. Racist police violence similarly spreads terror among racialised populations. Recognising that terror is part of how states function and maintain their power helps us identify the ideological role that the language of terrorism plays in disguising the origins of violence.

In fact, although 9/11 is portrayed as an exceptional moment in human history, it is not even exceptional within the late twentieth century. Its scale of destruction and death was experienced in its thousands by the people of Nicaragua, Cuba, Panama, the Middle East, North and Central Africa, Angola, South Africa, Indonesia, Sri Lanka, Vietnam, Afghanistan and Bosnia at the *hands* of the USA in the 1970s and 1980s.[12] And since 2001 it has been perpetrated almost continuously in Afghanistan, Iraq, Somalia, Pakistan, Kenya, Syria, Yemen and so many other places. As philosopher George Yancy also notes, from the perspective of Black Americans, '9/11 wasn't the first terror attack on American soil. Black people have known white terror throughout the history of this country',[13] and of course, the founding of the USA depended on mass genocide of Indigenous people.

---

11   https://opendemocracy.net/en/violence-comes-home-interview-with-arun-kundnani/ (accessed March 2021).

12   Chomsky, *Hegemony or Survival*.

13   https://truthout.org/articles/george-yancy-to-be-black-in-the-us-is-to-have-a-knee-against-your-neck-each-day/ (accessed August 2020).

'Muslim terrorist attacks' are not uniquely violent. They are portrayed to be because it is unthinkable to the white colonial imagination that attacks on civilians could occur anywhere other than in colonies and to racialised people. 'Over there', mass murder is a routine part of how the global economic system works to the advantage of the West. But there has always been one rule for the colonies, and another for the metropole.

Reductive explanations of terrorism also obscure the motives behind 'terrorist attacks' that take place outside of the West. Sometimes terms such as 'sectarianism' or 'Islamism' are invoked, but specific contexts and histories are glossed over. Instead, such violence is portrayed as natural and organic to non-Western geographies and their people.[14] This helps maintain an image of 'the Muslim world' that justifies constant Western intervention.

If we are serious about ending global violence, we cannot have a double standard about what we call it or when we care about it. Subsequently we must refrain from using the language of 'terrorism' as if it refers to something factual. All it does is obscure an inherently political conversation. Therefore, I refer to 'terrorism' and 'terrorist' in quotations throughout this book to consistently remind us that they are a narration, not a fact.

Resource theft

The War on Terror not only failed to end violence, but actively produced more. While this is distressing to anybody who places value on human life, such violence has been extremely beneficial to many stakeholders. In fact, the War on Terror has created endless new streams of profit through murder, dispossession and exploitation. To take an obvious example, it is an open secret

---

14   https://aljazeera.com/opinions/2021/8/18/monsters-inc-the-taliban-as-empires-bogeyman (accessed August 2021).

that the US invaded Iraq for oil. Before 2003 Iraq's oil industry was closed to Western companies – a fact noted by the CEO of Chevron in 1998 who said, 'Iraq possesses huge reserves of oil and gas, I'd love Chevron to have access to those reserves'.[15] Just over a decade later Iraq's oil fields were largely privately owned by Chevron, BP, Shell and ExxonMobil, robbing Iraqi people of a natural resource that might have made them one of the most self-sufficient countries in the world. As Republican Senator Chuck Hagel surmised, 'They talk about America's national interest. What the hell do you think they're talking about? We're not there for figs!'[16]

Indeed, Iraq's relation to the War on Terror was always tenuous. Reasons for invasion shifted from pre-empting President Saddam Hussein's use of Weapons of Mass Destruction, to concern for the human rights of Shias and Kurds, who had not been a concern when Iraq was considered a bulwark against the spread of the Iranian revolution. But this ambiguity is exactly the point. Because 'terrorism' was constructed as a racialised form of cultural/civilisational violence, the US could easily use it to frame Iraq as a space to be invaded. Despite bin Laden and Hussein being bitter enemies, by 2003 almost 50% of Americans thought Hussein was personally responsible for 9/11.[17] This enabled the US, with the UK, to launch their illegal occupation which led to the opening of Iraq's oil fields to Western markets. Islamophobia disguised this imperialist project as somehow heroic. But once Iraq was invaded, its major state institutions abolished, and oil privatised, there was effectively a return to the colonial relationship. And we only have to look at the rise of

15　https://edition.cnn.com/2013/03/19/opinion/iraq-war-oil-juhasz/index.html (accessed November 2020).

16　https://fpif.org/the_costs_of_war_for_oil/ (accessed August 2020).

17　Chomsky, *Hegemony or Survival*, p. 18.

IS today to see how such destabilisation of the region has gener-ated further violence which, ironically, is claimed to be simply a cultural/religious trait by the very Western powers whose inter-vention created the conditions for its rise.

In the Sahara-Sahel region the use of Islamophobia to justify imperialist theft has been even more blatant. US military pres-ence here also expanded in pursuit of oil, but 'the terrorist threat' it claimed to respond to is even more overtly fabricated. In 2003 the US colluded with Algerian secret military services to abduct 32 European tourists and then used the abduction to label the region a 'swamp of terror' that 'needs to be drained'.[18] Soon al-Qaeda bases were alleged to be spreading throughout the Sahara Desert, enabling US military to enter Senegal, Nigeria, Morocco, Tuni-sia and more. This helped them 'link together two of Africa's main oil- and gas-producing countries, Algeria and Nigeria, along with seven neighbouring Saharan-Sahelian states, into a military secu-rity arrangement whose architecture was American'.[19]

So, in the name of international security against 'the terror-ist threat', the US has established relations of colonial plunder and military domination around the world. Two decades after 9/11 they have 750 military bases in 80 countries costing over $50b a year.[20] In some places this presence is more disguised. For example in Kenya, the 'Rapid Response Team' is a suppos-edly indigenous national security response to al-Shabaab. But they are trained and formed by the CIA and Britain's MI6 who provide the intelligence they use to raid, detain and kill.[21]

---

18   Jeremy Keenan, 'Africa unsecured?', *Critical Studies on Terrorism*, Vol. 3, 2010, pp. 29–30.

19   Ibid., p. 31.

20   https://overseasbases.net/fact-sheet.html (accessed July 2021).

21   https://dailymaverick.co.za/article/2020-08-28-revealed-the-cia-and-mi6s-secret-war-in-kenya/ (accessed November 2020).

Western states and corporations are not the only beneficiaries either. Many 'Muslim countries' have also co-opted War on Terror language to justify repressing internal revolutions as 'quashing terrorist threats'. Some have also used the War on Terror's narrative to build lucrative alliances trading security technology and arms with Western governments. Additionally, as more peace deals are made between Gulf states and Israel, the language of 'security' and 'terrorism' continue to be used to delegitimise Palestinian resistance to occupation: Palestinians are cast as security threats and terrorists, while the Israeli state's project of settler colonialism is never spoken of in such terms.[22] Clearly, the Islamophobic construction of the figure of 'the terrorist' is essential both for justifying imperialism and for disguising it by labelling retaliation to it as purely non-political Muslim 'savagery'.

The business of war

Unlike Iraq and the Sahara-Sahel, the invasion of Afghanistan was declared as a direct response to the Taliban government's refusal to hand over bin Laden after 9/11. Backed by the UK, the US launched its invasion in 2001 with a bombing offensive in what was non-ironically named, Operation Enduring Freedom. Though Taliban forces were driven out of Kabul within six weeks, the UK and US only formally ceased operations in Afghanistan in August 2021. Furthermore, at the time of writing, the Taliban have regained government control in Kabul following the with-

---

22 For more on the occupation of Palestine see, Rashid Kahildi, *The Hundred Years' War on Palestine: A History of Settler Colonialism and Resistance, 1917–2017* (New York: Metropolitan Books, 2020); and https://decolonizepalestine.com/reading-list/ (accessed June 2021).

drawal of US troops, which throws into question the purpose of two decades of Western intervention.

Although Western corporations were not necessarily involved in directly siphoning raw materials from Afghanistan as they did in Iraq, this was largely due to lack of infrastructure. Indeed, in 2021 many Western commentators lamented the fact Afghanistan's natural mineral resources of copper, lithium and other rare elements have largely remained underground.[23] But war in Afghanistan was still a crucial source of profit through other avenues. Estimates suggest that in 2017 although only 9,800 US troops were on the ground, 26,000 Private Military Contractors (PMCs) were. PMCs are companies that sell armed combat services for profit. This billion-dollar industry benefits from drawn out wars that Western states would rather outsource, than admit failure over. UK-based companies such as G4S, Aegis Defence Services, Control Risks and Olive Group make hundreds of millions from such 'services'.[24] In Iraq, PMCs are hired to directly secure the operations of energy companies extracting oil – in other words, to defend their pillaging. This is reminiscent of the way the British East India Company built private militias to extract wealth from South Asia throughout the eighteenth and nineteenth centuries. As a former advisor to the World Bank put it, the War on Terror is 'merely an extension of defending the capitalist market'.[25]

Arms manufacturing companies have also done extraordinarily well in the War on Terror. The industry is supported by governments including the UK, who have approved £52b worth of arms sales and contracts since 2008 – £4.4b to the UK's own

23   https://edition.cnn.com/2021/08/18/business/afghanistan-lithium-rare-earths-mining/index.html (accessed August 2021).
24   Wendy Fitzgibbon & John Lea, *Privatising Justice*, (London: Pluto, 2020), p. 66.
25   Keenan, *Africa Unsecured*, p. 28.

list of 'countries of concern'.[26] 60% of arms sold went to states in the Middle East where many ended up in the hands of those Britain claims to ideologically oppose; once a weapon is sold there is no way to regulate who uses it or how it is used.[27] If the goal of security was to end global violence, there would be no place for arms companies and deals. Yet, states have facilitated billions of dollars' worth of private sales – particularly due to the advent of drone warfare.

Drones are remote-controlled technology that can be operated without people on the ground. This has proven very convenient since the 'boots on the ground' wars of Afghanistan and Iraq were costly to public image – drones hide much of the risk and violence of the War on Terror. Moreover, we are told they are more ethical tools of war because they use precise technology only targeting combatants. But according to the Bureau of Investigative Journalism, drone strikes in Afghanistan, Pakistan, Somalia and Yemen have killed between 8,500 to 12,000 civilians[28] – including Hawa's husband, as quoted at the beginning of this chapter. Even these estimates are conservative, though. After all, among a population racialised as terrorists, distinctions between combatant and civilian are blurred: a wedding becomes a training camp, a farmer carrying a spade becomes a terrorist with an air rifle.

Faheem Qureshi is a survivor of Barack Obama's first drone strike in 2009. The missile hit his home in Waziristan, a mountainous region in northern Pakistan bordering Afghanistan, killing everybody else and leaving 14 of his cousins fatherless, forcing him to drop out of school. He spent 40 days in hospital

26   https://caat.org.uk/data/exports-uk/ (accessed July 2021).

27   https://caat.org.uk/news/islam-and-the-uk-arms-trade/ (accessed July 2021).

28   https://thebureauinvestigates.com/projects/drone-war (accessed January 2021).

with shrapnel in his stomach, burns and lost one ear and eye. 'There are so many people like me in Waziristan that I know of who were targeted and killed . . . there is still no answer to this . . . there is not even acknowledgment that we were killed. They uproot us, they kill us, they target us without any reason. They turn our lives upside down'.[29] There are no formal procedures of inquiry into the deaths of civilians by drone, nor assistance or compensation afterwards.

In contrast, private defence companies like the British-based BAE Systems, as well as smaller tech and intelligence firms, make huge profits selling the technology and skills needed to kill by drone. This includes sales of armed and unarmed drones and surveillance planes which gather hours of video data, as well as providing analysists who look at footage to establish targets.[30] While it is military personnel who run operations, without private contractors drone-war could not exist as it does. Therefore companies directly profit from drone-war, making it a literal business of extracting value from the murder and maiming of racialised people. And although the US is associated with drone strikes more than the UK, the UK has its own drone programme and provides much of the intelligence for US strikes.

Prisoners of war

Drone warfare is only new in technique though, not principle. In the early years of the War on Terror, rather than assassinate by air, the CIA's Extraordinary Rendition programme would kidnap terror suspects from around the world and bring them

29   https://theguardian.com/world/2016/jan/23/drone-strike-victim-barack-obama (accessed January 2021).

30   https://theguardian.com/us-news/2015/jul/30/revealed-private-firms-at-heart-of-us-drone-warfare (accessed January 2021).

to secret military prisons where they could be tortured out of sight. Birmingham-born Moazzam Begg's experience of this is well known. He was seized by Pakistani intelligence in Pakistan, shortly after the invasion of Afghanistan in 2001 while he had been there building a school. They transferred Moazzam to US custody who held and tortured him first in Islamabad, then Kandahar and Bagram detention centres in Afghanistan, before Guantanamo Bay.

To call these places 'detention centres' puts it lightly. Detainees are given only the rights their captors decide to give them. As Moazzam tells me, 'I often say that Bush was the president of extrajudicial detention and Obama was the president of extrajudicial killing. They realised they could avoid being called human rights violators by prisoners giving testimony about what was done to them if they just killed people instead . . . That's why the drone programme has become so widespread.'

In US detention in Kandahar, Moazzam and others were stripped, beaten, abused and held in a barn where, 'other than the bullet holes from which we could look out, there was nothing you could see of natural light.'[31] And Bagram was the prison where Dilawar, a 22-year-old Afghan taxi driver and farmer was tortured to death because US soldiers found it amusing that when they hit him, he screamed, 'Allah'. There, Moazzam was deprived of sleep for a month in solitary confinement, interspersed with CIA-led interrogations and threats to his family.

Guantanamo Bay is the most notorious US military prison. It has never been shut down despite promises it would be and flagrant human rights abuses in front of a global audience for two decades. Moazzam was held there for three years before being released without charge or trial in 2005. Along with 14 other

---

31 https://nsarchive2.gwu.edu/torturingdemocracy/interviews/moazzam_begg. html (accessed January 2021).

British detainees he sued the British government for complicity in the torture they faced in US custody and received a financial compensation. But how do you put a price on the psychological, emotional, physical, and spiritual violence they faced?

Moazzam tells me,

> The last person was taken to Guantanamo in 2008 or 2009, but that part of the War on Terror is very much alive – there are still 40 prisoners at Guantanamo Bay who we're fighting for, who have not received any justice. A few of those were the very first prisoners there, they've been imprisoned for 20 years and never been charged with a crime. In 2014 the US Senate did a report on the CIA torture programme we experienced. That report is so huge they made Hollywood movies about it, but not a single person was prosecuted, and not a single torture survivor was asked for testimony.

Capitalism demands death

Ruth Wilson Gilmore defines racism as, 'the state-sanctioned . . . exploitation of group-differentiated vulnerability to premature death'.[32] The invasions, occupations, drone-strikes, torture, pillaging and economic catastrophe of the War on Terror, as well as its resulting starvation, homelessness and displacement have created blatant group-differentiated vulnerability to premature death for Muslims across the world. In Afghanistan, decades of conflict and civil war prior to 2001 made the country already vulnerable, but US and UK invasion led to the exacerbation of 'nearly every factor associated with premature death – poverty, malnutrition, poor sanitation, lack of access to health

---

32   Ruth Wilson Gilmore, *Golden Gulag: Prisons, Surplus, Crisis, and Opposition in Globalizing California* (California: University of California Press, 2007), p. 28.

care [and] environmental degradation';[33] hundreds of thousands have been killed.

One of the most catastrophic routes of exposure to premature death has come through the displacement caused by invasion and its accompanying climate catastrophes and regional conflict like the rise of IS. Today's so-called 'refugee crisis' is the consequence. At the time of writing, 37 million people have been displaced including 37% of Iraq's pre-war population, 26% of Afghanistan's, 37% of Syria's, 46% of Somalia's population, 1.7 million people in the Philippines, 3.5 million in Pakistan and on and on.[34] The mainstream discussion of these as humanitarian crises, often described by politicians and journalists as 'tragedies', fails to acknowledge that these are crises caused directly by capitalist projects of imperialism and the desire to profit from murder and theft. So although the language of security is used to justify technologies of war and foreign occupation, we must ask which of the millions of displaced people across the world has been made more secure by the War on Terror?

Since 2001 the language of terrorism and defeating 'the Muslim terrorist', has enabled Western states to hide and depoliticise histories of racial violence and contexts of imperialist profit-making which non-state actors' attacks often respond to. Islamophobia is not only the racism that enables this, Islamophobia is also its outcome. Muslims across the world are killed and engulfed by lethal and disabling conditions because of racialised economic plunder and an industry of war. Part of resisting

---

33 https://watson.brown.edu/costsofwar/costs/human/civilians/afghan#:~:text=Prior%20wars%20and%20civil%20conflict,reduced%20access%20to%20health%20care (accessed January 2021).

34 David Vine et al., *Creating Refugees: Displacement Caused by the United States' Post 9/11 Wars* (Rhode Island: Brown University, 2020), p. 17.

this system of colonialism, capitalism and white supremacy involves recognising *it* as the source of violence.

Pursuit of 'international security' through the War on Terror has not made our world safer, it has enhanced experiences of terror, violence and indignity for the global majority. The only thing that has been secured is the profit and hegemony of Western corporations and the states that facilitate their ventures. To even begin a conversation about building a safer world we must reject this notion of security altogether and end the Islamophobic War on Terror.

Chapter 3

Who is safer when the nation is secure?

When they took her father away, my daughter, Ruqayyah, was two years old. She witnessed it all. She didn't know many words then, just some children's words in Arabic, like Didi. Didi meant getting hurt. She kept putting her hands together, to gesture the handcuffs they'd had her Abi in, and saying 'Abi didi, Abi didi!' – they're hurting Abi, they're hurting Abi.[1]
– Celeste

The above testimony comes from Celeste, a Senegalese-French woman who moved to the UK aged 17. Her husband was born in Algeria and came to the UK to study. They settled here and gave birth to their daughter, Ruqayyah. Ruqayyah's Abi's arrest took place in 2001 on terrorism-related charges that he was never given evidence or put on trial for. Nonetheless, he was held in high-security solitary confinement for five years – leaving him wheelchair-bound and suicidal. Then he was put under house-arrest until being re-arrested, re-imprisoned, threatened with deportation and back under house-arrest until 2013, when charges against him were dropped. By then the family's life was changed forever.

---

1 Not their real names, testimony is from, https://hhugs.org.uk/2019/05/celeste-story-part-1/ (accessed November 2020).

The term 'national security' evokes James Bond-esque spies, bomb-defusing heroes who save the nation, and villains whose plots must be foiled. But Ruqayyah's family's story reveals the reality of the razor-edged tangled web that is the national security system. National security and counterterror-related laws have been passed annually since 2000 in the UK and presented as essential to keep us safe. On paper, they look like a neat chronological list, but the ways they interact with and trap people in cycles of psychological, economic and physical violence, is anything but neat and linear. So, who do they keep safe, and at whose cost?

While the last chapter explored how security measures against the racialised 'terrorist threat' have enabled global oppression and exploitation, here I turn to the violence inflicted in its name within Western nation-states. Although I focus on Britain, the patterns of policy-making and coercion described are taking place across many states in the name of security, and the conclusions we can draw from this are similar.

I relay Celeste's story above from the account she gave to HHUGS (Helping Households Under Great Stress). HHUGS are the only UK charity supporting families impacted by counterterrorism policies. They tell me how most families they work with endure similar experiences. 'It often starts with a male family member getting arrested following a traumatic dawn-raid by police'. They describe how dozens of armed officers invade family homes, searching and stripping every corner, taking everything from laptops and phones, to books, Qurans, glasses prescriptions and medicine. Celeste recounted them even inspecting Ruqayyah's nappies – the suspicion attached to 'Muslimness' extends to our most banal possessions.

HHUGS continue, 'Following the raid, families' financial assets are frozen at times, which, alongside the arrest, leave many without a source of income, access to savings or recourse to public funds.' Some HHUGS clients have even had disability benefits stopped after raids.[2] As a result, they often 'have to choose between heating their homes and eating – some tell us they would have ended up homeless without our support.' This economic terrorisation by the state 'affects people emotionally and is amplified by the fact they're often ostracised from community and even family members who do not want to be associated.' Loud dawn raids by militarised police not only terrorise the family they raid – they deliberately instil wider fear.

During the raid on Ruqayyah's home, Celeste's husband was arrested on terrorism-related charges. This type of arrest may sound straightforward, but the reality of terrorism charges are surprisingly ambiguous. The UK's counterterror laws rest on similar racialised assumptions to the War on Terror: the Crown Prosecution Service states, 'terrorism offences are distinct from other types of crime' with motives 'unlike typical criminal motivations'.[3] Subsequently, terrorism offences are seen to require special forms of policing and punishment beyond what the criminal justice system usually includes. For example, terrorism laws allow police to detain you without charge for up to 14 days,[4] freeze your bank account,[5] restrict who you can see, where you go and more. This effectively creates a 'parallel criminal justice system' that impacts mainly Muslims.[6] But we must realise this

---

2   https://hhugs.org.uk/2018/05/walids-story/ (accessed November 2020).

3   https://cps.gov.uk/crime-info/terrorism (accessed December 2020).

4   https://gov.uk/arrested-your-rights/how-long-you-can-be-held-in-custody (accessed December 2020).

5   https://gov.uk/government/publications/quarterly-report-to-parliament-1-october-2020-to-31-december-2020-tafa-2010/quarterly-report-to-parliament-1-october-2020-to-31-december-2020-tafa-2010 (accessed March 2021).

6   Arun Kundnani et al., *Leaving the War on Terror* (Amsterdam: Transnational Institute, 2019), p. 30.

has also expanded the possibility for such powers to seep into broader policing, too.

Such rules and restrictions come from laws that build on the Terrorism Act 2000. Terrorism was legally defined by this act as, 'the use or threat of action' that is designed to 'influence governments', 'intimidate the public' or 'advance a political, religious, racial [added in 2008] or ideological cause'. In this definition, 'action' is defined as 'serious violence against a person', 'serious damage to property', 'serious risk' to somebody's life or to the safety or health of a group of people.[7] It also includes actions taken 'for the benefit of proscribed organisations' classified as organisations that 'commit', 'prepare for', 'promote or encourage' or are 'otherwise concerned in terrorism'.[8] 'Support' for such organisations could be in 'opinion or belief', wearing 'an item of clothing' associated with them or through funding.[9]

This definition of terrorism is so broad and vague that even the Supreme Court judged it unsatisfactory in 2012.[10] It criminalises activities most of us would not consider terrorism, let alone harmful. For example, people resisting an oppressive government that is the UK's strategic ally, could be classed as 'a proscribed organisation' and therefore terrorists. And by this definition, you would not have to even be part of the organisation to be considered a terrorist. Simply learning about, donating to or speaking in favour of them could count as a terrorism offence. This primarily affects people fleeing political

---

7   https://legislation.gov.uk/ukpga/2000/11/section/1#commentary-c16756551 (accessed March 2021).

8   https://legislation.gov.uk/ukpga/2000/11/section/3#commentary-c16756551 (accessed March 2021).

9   Ibid.

10   Alan Greene, 'The Quest for a Satisfactory Definition of Terrorism: R v Gul', *The Modern law Review*, Vol. 77:5, 2014, pp. 780–93.

persecution, because the UK government frames *them* as dangerous, not the conditions they flee.[11]

For example, human rights lawyer, Gareth Peirce, has spoken about how this broad classification affected Algerian refugees involved in self-defence efforts against government massacres in the 1990s and early 2000s. Having fled Algeria, many of them were charged under the Terrorism Act in the UK for their resistance efforts which were classed as membership of 'proscribed organisations'.[12] This criminalised their self-defence against Algerian state violence and doubly punished those seeking political asylum. Given that Celeste's husband was from Algeria, he may have faced similar charges – although his charges remain unknown even to him, as we shall come to. In any case, it is crucial to ask whether a state with imperialist foreign policy should get to decide which international struggles are legitimate, and if this should fall under 'countering terrorism'.

The fact you do not have to act violently to be convicted under terrorism laws is surprising to most people. When, in Britain in 2017, the Stansted 15 tried to stop a deportation flight removing people from UK detention to Nigeria, Ghana and Sierra Leone by locking on to each other to prevent use of the plane, their charge was changed from a minor public order offence to a terror-related offence which, under terrorism laws, meant 'even encouraging the actions of Stansted 15 would constitute a criminal offence'.[13] Although they won their appeal, the point stands that the state's definition of 'terrorism' can be used to criminalise both people fleeing political persecution, and those

---

11   Liz Fekete, 'The Terrorism Act 2000: An Interview with Gareth Peirce', *Race & Class*, Vol. 43:2, 2001, 95–103, p. 98.

12   Ibid., p. 101.

13   https://hja.net/news-and-insights/press-releases/criminal-defence/court-of-appeal-quashes-terror-charges-of-stansted-15/ (accessed February 2021).

acting in solidarity with them, and therefore any number of other actions, words or ideas. This repressive situation is broadly accepted by wider society because people imagine it keeps us safe against the threat of Muslim terrorists. But national security measures expand the state's powers to repress more broadly at its own discretion. So, although the apparatus has been built on the back of Islamophobia, it threatens even those who consent to it.

Criminal ideas

75% of people in prison for terrorism-related offences in the UK are categorised as 'holding Islamist-extremist views'.[14] In these cases, they have not acted violently, but because of how they are racialised, their ideas are deemed dangerous. Their imprisonment is made possible by Section 5 of the 2006 Terrorism Act that makes it an offence to 'engage in preparation' for acts of terrorism.[15] Preparation for terrorism may sound like it relates to stockpiling explosives, but in Peirce's experience defending such cases, evidence for 'preparation' is usually found 'after a search on the defendant's computer or in a notebook'. This includes poems they have written,[16] documents read,[17] or internet search histories.[18] Possession or perusal of such literature is said to show

---

14 https://gov.uk/government/statistics/operation-of-police-powers-under-the-terrorism-act-2000-quarterly-update-to-december-2020/operation-of-police-powers-under-the-terrorism-act-2000-and-subsequent-legislation-arrests-outcomes-and-stop-and-search-great-britain-year-ending (accessed 22 March 2021).
15 https://bbc.co.uk/news/uk-50823532 (accessed March 2021).
16 For example see the 'Lyrical Terrorist', https://theguardian.com/uk/2008/jun/17/uksecurity.ukcrime (accessed March 2021).
17 See the case of Rizwaan Sabir, discussed below.
18 Gareth Peirce, 'Was it like this for the Irish?', *London Review of Books*, Vol. 30:7, 2008.

'desire to incite, encourage or glorify terrorism'.[19] This extraordinary claim assumes that engaging with an idea obliges you to act upon it. On this basis, schools should never teach about Nazism, slavery or any historic violence.

Enabling the state to judge which ideas are acceptable to read or write about gives it a blank cheque to censor ideas that threaten to expose its violence. This does not make us safer. After all, cabinet ministers who plan to cut benefits and leave people homeless are not considered to be preparing for acts which pose a serious risk to the health and safety of a section of the public. Nor are Home Office employees who prepare border controls that create conditions of serious risk for migrants and refugees. Instead, most terrorism-related convictions in the last decade were of Muslims who have been charged for 'preparatory activity' which, in lawyer David Gottleib's words, tends to mean that they are 'terrorist by negligence' – they read or downloaded something. Consenting to this persecution of Muslims allows the state's grip on power to become more secure for abuse, while its terrorisation of marginalised people at home and abroad is hidden.

The terror of endless suspicion

Counterterror policing is not a one-time event, its repercussions can last a lifetime. As Rizwaan Sabir tells me, 'once you're categorised as a "subject of interest" for suspected terrorism, it can become quite difficult to become uninteresting'. He mentions this in relation to the way that people who face terrorism charges continue to be hounded by counterterror policing throughout their lives even when such charges are dropped, as they often are.

---

19 Ibid.

In 2008 Rizwaan was studying for his MA at the University of Nottingham and downloaded the al-Qaeda training manual from the US Department of Justice website for his research about terrorism. After the document was found on a University computer he was arrested under Terrorism powers and detained for a week in degrading conditions of police custody without any charges.[20] Over a decade later, now an activist and academic, Rizwaan reflects,

> the moment you're arrested and taken into custody, the police begin to see and construct you as being dangerous because of your racialised Muslim identity . . . This suspicion doesn't just disappear the moment you're released without charge from custody but follows you for years to come. For me, it came through a whole series of stops and searches at the roadside, detentions at air and land ports when I travelled or returned to the UK, and of course, a whole series of intelligence entries that were being logged by the police. All these things reinforce a sense of trauma in your psyche and follow you around in daily life in multiple ways.

These constant interventions and surveillance demonstrate that the web of national security is its own form of terror. Like Rizwaan, Celeste's husband continued experiencing Terrorism policing after release from prison. For him, this came through a Control Order – part of the 2005 Terrorism Act that morphed into Terrorism Prevention and Investigation Measures (TPIMs) in 2011. Control Orders and TPIMs impose devastating restraints on a person's life in the name of 'preventing' violence.[21] Celeste's

20   https://legislation.gov.uk/ukpga/2000/11/section/41 (accessed March 2021).
21   David Anderson, Control Orders in 2011: Final Report of the Independent Reviewer on the Prevention of Terrorism Act 2005 (London: The Stationery Office, 2012).

husband was tagged and not allowed to leave his house or let anybody in from outside without clearance. This turned home into a prison and even transformed everyday chores like boiler repairs into security issues because 'everyone who came to the house had to . . . submit their passport to the Home Office.' Additionally, Celeste's husband had to check-in with the tagging company five times a day, and even still, somebody from the Home Office would come round 'every 2 or 3 days – even at 1 and 2am in the morning to check.'[22] Such deliberate disruption left the family unable to live peacefully *at* home, let alone to leave it. Yet, despite being forcibly homebound, he was re-arrested after several years and threatened with deportation.

Such constant surveillance and threat of policing has profound psychological impacts. It left Celeste's family traumatised. Despite never being convicted of anything, Celeste's husband was held in a cell for 23 hours a day in Belmarsh prison which eventually led him to stop eating and speaking. He made multiple suicide attempts and left prison using a wheelchair. At the same time, Celeste experienced frequent hospitalisation for panic attacks and Ruqayyah, their daughter, 'was always scared and crying . . . if I left her alone for one minute . . . she would start screaming immediately . . .'[23]

In Rizwaan's case, although 13 years have passed since his detention, he has never stopped experiencing 'acute paranoia' and 'crippling anxiety that follows me everywhere I go . . . sometimes it's gotten too much and I've ended up falling quite unwell with serious mental health and psychiatric problems . . . but I've struggled to draw on the help of the NHS because I know the public sector is under a legal duty to pass intelligence to the police'.

---

22   https://hhugs.org.uk/2019/05/celeste-story-part-2/ (accessed November 2020).
23   https://hhugs.org.uk/2019/05/celeste-story-part-1/ (accessed November 2020).

Indeed, the national security system not only directly targets people but also undermines their access to possible healing from it due to the prevalence of Prevent and counter-extremism policing, explored in the following chapters. Those parts of the security web mean that if Rizwaan was to tell an NHS therapist that the cause of his anxiety is counterterror policing, they would likely refer him *back* to the counterterrorism apparatus as suspicious. Similarly, children whose parents are charged under terrorism legislation are often monitored by social services for being 'at risk of radicalisation'. This criminalises them for the trauma they have experienced from police raids and the state-induced poverty that cause PTSD.

These cycles of state abuse are largely ignored by the wider public because of widespread belief in a barbaric, fanatic, Muslim Other who likely deserves such policing. Or, since its victims are primarily Muslims with precarious financial and immigration statuses, nobody cares about them. But if the only way we can imagine living safely involves enacting massive levels of endless violence against marginalised people, something is very wrong.

Imprisoned by terror

Nonetheless, the state's system of violence is more often expanded than restricted, even when it obviously fails. For example, in 2020 the Counter-Terrorism and Sentencing Bill was passed to extend prison sentences for people convicted of preparatory activity for terrorism, and to end early release. The justification for the bill was the murder of Jack Merritt and Saskia Jones by Usman Khan, a former prisoner at a rehabili-tation event in London in 2019. These murders were cynically used to enlarge the policing system instead of proving its inef-fectiveness for tackling violence. After all, Usman had already been through prison, Terrorism policing, surveillance and a 'counter-extremism' programme.

Some misguided opposition to the bill suggested that keeping terrorism-offenders in prison longer would further 'radicalise' them because prisons are 'sites of radicalisation'. But this argument in fact criminalises Muslim prisoners further and leads to measures like 'extremist wings' that segregate them based on the idea that violence is a Muslim contagion. Muslims already make up over 15%[24] of the UK prison population. 40% are Asian and 32% Black.[25] Only 1% are there on terrorism charges, the rest are there due to historic over-policing of working-class Black and brown people that allows the state to avoid addressing the socioeconomic conditions that produce 'crime'. Nonetheless, all incarcerated Muslims are hyper-criminalised due to the terrorist trope and consequently experience more harm.

For example, guards are more likely to restrain and segregate Muslim prisoners.[26] Islam is routinely weaponised against them, too. Social justice charity, Maslaha, found that despite breaching regulation, many Muslims are regularly banned from attending Jummah (Friday prayers) as punishment.[27] The climate of suspicion also means Muslims cannot trust prison welfare services despite facing additional mental strain. Consequently, many find comfort in Islam and among Muslim peers. But management see such bonding itself as 'radicalisation'. One formerly-imprisoned

---

24 David Lammy, The Lammy Review, (UK: UK Government, 2017).

25 HM Chief Inspector of Prisons, 'Muslim prisoners' experiences: A thematic review (UK: HMP, 2010), p. 4.

26 Ibid; and see Darrick Jolliffe and Zubaida Haque, *Have prisons become a dangerous place? Disproportionality, safety and mental health in British prisons* (London: Runnymede, 2017); and https://theguardian.com/society/2017/oct/19/black-and-muslim-prisoners-suffer-worse-treatment-study-finds (accessed January 2021).

27 Raheel Mohammed & Lauren Nickolls, *Time to end the silence: The experience of Muslims in the prison system* (London: Maslaha, 2020).

Muslim man told Maslaha, 'praying five times a day in congregation is normal and it happens every day . . . but when it happens in a prison environment and you've got a bunch of Muslim lads in one cell, it starts setting off alarms in the prison staff – what are they up to, what's going on?'[28] Islamophobia not only justifies imprisonment of Muslims then, it further criminalises those *in* prison, undermining their chances *after* prison and certainly not lessening the likelihood of violence, as Usman Khan showed.

The solution is not more 'BAME police and prison staff' as some have suggested.[29] If history teaches us anything, it's that no matter the number of reviews, reforms and new faces in the policing system, there will always be a need for more because they do not address the fundamental issue: the system is not broken, it is meant to work this way.[30] In Angela Davis' words, 'Prisons do not disappear social problems, they disappear human beings. Homelessness, unemployment, drug addiction, mental illness, and illiteracy are only a few of the problems that disappear from public view when the human beings contending with them are relegated to cages.'[31] Instead of reforming a system built on and justified by racism and Islamophobia, we need to demand different conditions altogether. Policing and prison do not make us safer.

Secret evidence and citizenship removal

The threat to deport Celeste's husband after years of imprisonment illustrates the overlap between immigration legislation

28   Ibid., p. 16.

29   See for example, https://theguardian.com/society/2017/oct/19/black-and-muslim-prisoners-suffer-worse-treatment-study-finds (accessed January 2021).

30   Mariame Kaba, *We Do This 'til We Free Us: Abolitionist Organizing and Transforming Justice* (Chicago: Haymarket Books, 2021), p. 5.

31   http://historyisaweapon.com/defcon1/davisprison.html (accessed January 2021).

and national security policing. While 'evidence' in most terrorism-related charges is baseless, in cases like Celeste's husband's, the evidence is actually kept secret. Use of secret evidence began at the Special Immigration Appeals Commission (SIAC) established in 1997. SIAC deals with deportations of people with foreign nationalities and citizenship removal of British nationals on national security grounds. In these cases, the state's evidence is not shared with you or your lawyer because it could damage 'the interests of national security'. In addition, neither of you can enter the court room when the trial takes place. Instead, a 'Special Advocate' vetted by the court, will represent you but cannot speak to you once they have seen the evidence, and therefore cannot take further instruction on points it raises.[32]

Fahad Ansari is a lawyer who has defended many people faced with SIAC proceedings. He tells me, 'It is disarming enough to be told you represent such a threat to national security that the state will strip you of your citizenship and leave you effectively stateless in a foreign country; however, to not be shown or told of the evidence against you to be able to challenge it results in feelings of complete and utter helplessness . . . some equate the process with fighting ghosts.'

Despite how unjust such proceedings are, since 2013 they have expanded into civil cases including family and employment tribunals, meaning people can lose jobs or children based on secret evidence.[33] This demonstrates how expansion of state powers in the name of 'exceptional' security cases deliberately

---

32 https://kingsleynapley.co.uk/insights/blogs/public-law-blog/judicial-review-and-the-creep-of-closed-material-procedures-r-on-the-application-of-haralambous-v-crown-court-at-st-albans-and-another (accessed March 2021).

33 Jessie Blackbourn, 'Closed material procedures in the radicalisation cases,' *Child and Family Law Quarterly*, Vol. 32:4, 2020; and John Sullivan, 'Closed Material Procedures and the Right to a Fair Trial', *Maryland Journal of International Law*, Vol. 29:1, 2014.

opens the possibility of such abuses being normalised. In fact, Moazzam Begg told me, 'I call this the "Guantanamo-isation of legislation" whereby countries which proclaim open and transparent justice systems have now normalised secret evidence which began in Guantanamo tribunals but has now become widespread'. Far from just a 'Muslim issue', the right to a fair trial becomes increasingly conditional for all; as does assurance of citizenship.

Over 70 people were stripped of citizenship through SIAC between 2002–16, and 104 in 2017 alone. Since 2014, the process became easier with the Home Secretary only needing to be 'satisfied' a person could receive citizenship 'elsewhere' for a removal to go ahead.[34] This heightens the vulnerability of racialised people since we will always be assumed to belong 'elsewhere'.

Many of us know the details of Shamima Begum's case because of the Islamophobic fever that gripped the media in 2018. Shamima was so reviled by British press that making a 20-year-old stateless was deemed 'the right thing to do'. The Home Secretary was satisfied that Shamima, whose parents were born in Bangladesh, would be able to apply for Bangladeshi citizenship. But having no allegiance to her, Bangladesh refused, meaning that removal of her British citizenship left her stateless in a refugee camp with three children dead. In 2021 the UK's highest court ruled she could not even come back to appeal her case due to 'security concerns'.[35] The violence Shamima represents is therefore portrayed as worse than the violence she has faced not only at the hands of the state, but when, as a 15-year-old child, she was the victim of IS grooming and statutory rape.

---

34   https://independent.co.uk/news/uk/home-news/isis-brides-reema-iqbal-zara-syria-uk-citizenship-shamima-begum-home-office-sajid-javid-a8816221.html (accessed November 2020).

35   https://aljazeera.com/opinions/2021/3/19/shamima-begum-british-citizenship (accessed March 2021).

Reports from 2020 found that tens of British women and many more children are in a similar position to Shamima. They are systematically deprived of citizenship and left stateless in camps in the Syrian region.[36] Twenty-five people die a month in these camps from dehydration, malnutrition and hypothermia, and guards shoot and sexually abuse detainees. The British state directly enables this violence through citizenship removals, but by invoking Islamophobia through 'national security concerns', the wider public relieve it of all responsibility. Where can these women apply for recourse to justice and who has been made safer by exposing them to so much harm?

Policing the Other 'at home'

It is tempting to think of the measures covered in this chapter as an outcome of the state becoming authoritarian or fascist. But rather than signalling a mutation of the 'healthy' 'usual' working of Britain's democracy and criminal justice system, it is truer to understand national security policing as the outcome of the colonial history British democracy is founded upon. In that history, the racialised Other was defined as inherently lawless and guilty to justify slavery, occupation, theft and genocide.

Therefore, although the counterterror police who raided Ruqayyah's home present a very different image of policing to the 'bobby on the beat', this is not because counterterror policing disrupts standard policing procedure. Instead, there have been two tiers of policing for as long as the British state has policed. One, 'at home' since the late 1800s, to protect capitalist interests against working-class people who were beginning to unionise to resist exploitative working conditions. The second form

36 https://rightsandsecurity.org/impact/entry/europes-guantanamo-report (accessed March 2021).

developed in the colonies to repress widespread resistance to British rule – this was counterinsurgency policing. So, although counterterror laws technically create a 'parallel system' of punishments from the 'normal' criminal justice system, this simply mirrors the fact Britain has always used a second system to discipline racialised Others.

Indeed, techniques Britain used to hold onto colonies in South Asia, Kenya, Malaya (Singapore), West Africa, Ireland, South Africa and many other places, look very similar to counterterror policing today. This included militarised police units, armed raids, infiltration of resistance, false arrest, blockades, destruction of homes, concentration camps and murder to crush anti-colonial resistance and deter others from it.[37] Those who resisted were labelled terrorists, rebels and rioters to justify policing aimed at suppression.

In the second half of the twentieth century, these tactics were recognised as powerful forms of repression and adopted by COINTELPRO, the US's 'Counterintelligence Program'. They used these techniques to destroy and fracture anti-war groups, left-wing organisations and, notoriously, Black Liberation groups like the Black Panthers – who were spied on, subject to misinformation campaigns, mass arrest and assassination. In Britain, COINTELPRO tactics have used undercover policing, deceptive long-term relationships, and stolen identities from dead children to spy on people deemed 'problems for the state'.[38]

But more visible counterinsurgency techniques began to be used in Britain when Black and brown communities and their

---

37 Laleh Khalili, *Time in the Shadows: Confinement in Counterinsurgencies* (California: Stanford University Press, 2012), p. 9.

38 https://theguardian.com/uk-news/2014/jul/24/special-demonstration-squad-undercover-unit-analysis (accessed March 2021); and see, https://www.spycops.co.uk/ (accessed March 2021).

anti-racist movements grew larger, particularly by the 1980s. For instance, after anti-racist uprisings in Brixton, Toxteth, Leeds and elsewhere in 1981, the Met Police appointed a Commissioner who had previously worked for the British Palestine police and headed the Royal Ulster Constabulary – the violent militarised police force used by Britain in Northern Ireland. In his own words, colonial policing taught him that policing was less about 'crime prevention' and more about 'social control'.[39] Therefore, methods previously used to ensure Britain's grip on its colonies were readjusted and applied within Britain itself to put the ex-colonised in their place.

Far from undermining Britain's otherwise impartial legal system, national security and counterterrorism policing grow out of this colonial history. Therefore, it is not enough that we repeal all counterterror laws. Resisting the foundations of Islamophobia demands uprooting liberalism's inherently racialised ideas about law and policing in the first place. Far from universal and enlightened, those ideas depend on an always-already-guilty racial Other imagined as lawless and violent.

Social control and deterrence

While most Muslims may not have first-hand experience of our homes being raided, citizenship stripped or prison, the national security web still weaves in and out of our lives to 'keep us in check'. Take Schedule 7 of the Terrorism Act 2000. This gives police power to stop, search, question and detain (for up to six hours) anyone travelling through or into the UK, to establish if they have been involved in preparing, supporting or executing acts of terrorism.

---

39   James Trafford, *The Empire at Home: Internal Colonies and the End of Britain* (London: Pluto, 2020), p. 67.

419,000 people were stopped under Schedule 7 between 2009–19. Since no 'reasonable grounds for suspicion' are needed for these stops,[40] they result in racial profiling so familiar that every Muslim comedian has a sketch about it and most Muslims set off early to the airport in anticipation. We could fixate on how ineffective this discrimination is. Only 0.007% of stops lead to terrorism convictions despite the broad definition of the term.[41] But such focus accepts the state's claim that the law aims to prosecute terrorists. Instead, Schedule 7 is a tool of mass surveillance, data collection and disciplining.

It is illegal for you to remain silent if you're stopped under Schedule 7. You must answer questions, submit luggage for searching, provide DNA and fingerprints, and give passwords to electronic devices. These alarming powers disregard usual international privacy laws threatening the work of lawyers, journalists and activists. For example, in 2018 Mohammed Rabbani, international director of human rights organisation CAGE, was arrested and charged with obstructing police because he refused to give the passwords to his devices as they held 30,000 documents of sensitive legal information about torture victims.[42]

But even for those of us without such sensitive information on our phones, Schedule 7 enforces self-policing. For example, I was filled with fear after hearing stories of Muslim women who were threatened with arrest if they refused to remove their hijabs for photographs under Schedule 7. To avoid anything similar happening to me I delete all social media apps before entering the airport, wipe text conversations, and make sure not to carry

---

40   Home Office, Review of the Operation of Schedule 7: A Public Consultation, (London: UK Home Office: 2012).

41   https://cage.ngo/schedule-7-harassment-at-borders-report-executive-summary (accessed March 2021).

42   https://bbc.co.uk/news/uk-41394156 (accessed March 2021).

any literature related to 'controversial' political issues. This is not because I 'have something to hide' or am in the midst of a 'terror-plot' in the group chat, instead it is the deliberate effect of Schedule 7's coercion. Laws that target on an Islamophobic basis deliberately discourage Muslims from participating in political critique more broadly. They aim to pacify us by making us feel the apparatus is too big to resist. Subsequently, most of us normalise and adjust our lives to it. But that means sacrificing our right to live freely as political beings.

This is a form of social control and it is not limited to Schedule 7. In fact, a powerful tool of deterring people from political critique or resistance to the state is through undercover policing and intelligence operations. Lots of us have heard of people testifying that the MI5 asked them to spy on fellow Muslims in mosques, youth clubs and elsewhere – or even to convert to Islam to get inside.[43] In many cases these demands are backed by the threat of arrest, citizenship removal or deportation. Even just knowing that the state seeks to secretly police our communities enforces self-policing and wariness. Especially when we hear of the well-documented use of entrapment.

Entrapment cases use undercover police to encourage people to participate in or say something that can be used to arrest them for preparatory activity. In the case of Munir Farooqi, who ran an Islamic da'wah book stall in Manchester, he was convicted under 'preparatory activity' for terrorism based on answers he gave two undercover officers who approached him pretending to be new Muslims and asking him leading questions.[44] The counterterror chief in this case admitted, 'This was an extremely challenging case to prosecute . . . because we did not recover any

---

43   Peirce, 'Was it like this for the Irish?', p. 8.
44   https://cage.ngo/munir-farooqi-2 (accessed March 2021).

blueprint, attack plan or endgame . . .'[45] Clearly, the strategies used by intelligence services demonstrate the state *creating* the very 'terrorists' it claims to counter in order to justify its policies.

Nonetheless, knowing that something found on you in a Schedule 7 stop, or said to an undercover officer, could be used to charge you with 'preparatory activity' for terrorism, or as 'secret evidence' to revoke your citizenship, is beyond frightening. It forces Muslims to internalise Islamophobia and review our actions, words and thoughts on a basis of how they could appear to the state's practice of racialised policing. Consequently, the state does not need to raid all of our homes or stop and search every one of us. Instead, we take on the responsibility of monitoring our words, actions and online behaviour to avoid anything that could be seen as 'suspicious'. This is deliberately depoliticising and pacifying. Hajera Begum, an activist with Abolitionist Futures, described the feeling as 'choking'. She tells me, 'it makes it very difficult to even try and organise against wider societal issues such as racism, fascism and capitalism'.

No justice, no peace

To build societies counter to violence, we first need justice. As a bare minimum that requires repealing all national security and counterterror legislation and all policing systems that criminalise and punish ideas, speech, actions and identities. We imagine we need policing and security measures to deal with violence, but such measures do not confront the primary source of violence in our society, which is the state that attacks, starves, exploits, cages, exiles and destroys lives for the profit of private interests, through trapping people in cycles of violence.

---

45 https://bbc.co.uk/news/uk-england-manchester-14851811 (accessed March 2021).

Yet such state and structural violence is hidden by Islamophobic focus on 'the Muslim terrorist'. Islamophobia therefore obscures the fact that so much of what security measures claim to address would be much better dealt with through ending the conditions of racism, imperialism and capitalism that give rise to violence. That is not only a task of repealing and abolition, but of creatively and collectively imagining new ways to create ecosystems of well-being with routes to address harm that centre the most marginalised, rather than punish them, and which envision an entirely different framework for thinking about justice.

Islamophobia limits our ability to imagine alternatives because the majority of liberal, democratic societies who profess love for rule of law and freedom of speech would rather consent to state repression and terror, than divest from imagining Muslims as backwards, barbaric, terrorists. Not only is this racist; it is futile. In the words of James Baldwin, to Angela Davis, 'if they take you in the morning, they will be coming for us that night.' Muslims may be disproportionately targeted and trapped in the web of national security policing today, but that webbing is being silently spun through every fibre of society, encroaching on all possible future dissent to the state's agenda. Focus on 'Muslim threat' is a deliberate distraction.

Chapter 4

Racist prediction as public duty: Prevent

Adam was eight years old when counterterrorism police interrogated him.[1] He wasn't being held at a police station or stopped at the border, Adam was interrogated at primary school. His teacher took him to a classroom just after lunch, where three adults he had never met were waiting for him: two counterterrorism officers and a social worker. She left him alone with them. They asked whether he liked school, and what games he played at home. Did he play them with his father? Which relatives did they visit? Did he pray? Go to mosque? What did he read at mosque? The officers asked Adam if he could recite some of the Quran in Arabic and then asked if he knew the meaning of the words. Apparently, they were looking to have a theological discussion with an eight-year-old.

When Adam's mum came to collect him, his teacher informed her that Adam was being questioned by police and she, too, would have to speak to them. Why had nobody told her? Was Adam okay? The officers did not greet or give their names to Adam's mum. Instead, they asked why she thought the London Bridge attack and 7/7 had happened. She suggested, maybe it

---

1   Not his real name. Story reported by PreventWatch in 2018, https://preventwatch. org/the-quran-case-prevent-crossing-the-red-line/ (accessed July 2020).

had something to do with the Middle East? 'No, it's all happening because of the Quran', they told her.

Shortly after Adam and his mum finally arrived at home, the officers followed. Adam cowered behind his grandad as they interrogated his dad, repeatedly asking if he 'wants the UK to become an Islamic country'. After they left, Adam did not tell his parents the details of his interrogation for a week. What thoughts were going through his eight-year-old mind? Did he think he was in trouble? That he had done something wrong at school? That his teacher didn't like him?

Weeks later, unannounced, the social worker revisited Adam's home to inform them that he had been investigated for 'radicalisation concerns' under Prevent, but that his case was now closed. She did not apologise or expand. What were these radicalisation concerns about? Who had raised them and on what basis? Why was the case dropped? Would the referral affect Adam's future schooling? What did the police do with his information? Where was it stored?

Such questions are left unanswered not only for Adam, but for thousands of children reported to Prevent by teachers, doctors or other public servants since 2015. In fact, people under 20 made up 54% of Prevent referrals between 2019–20,[2] and between 2015–18, 532 children under the age of six were referred.[3] The basis of child referrals can seem preposterous. In 2021, a four-year-old was referred for talking about the popular video game, Fortnite, saying he had 'guns and bombs in his shed';[4]

---

2   Home Office, 'Individuals referred to and supported through the Prevent programme', Home Office statistics release bulletin 36/20 (London: UK Home Office, 2020), p. 9.

3   https://thetimes.co.uk/article/children-under-6-referred-to-extremism-programme-c3vlzf56s (accessed July 2021).

4   https://theguardian.com/uk-news/2021/jan/31/muslim-boy-4-was-referred-to-prevent-over-game-of-fortnite (accessed March 2021).

and when an eleven-year-old told his class he hoped to give 'alms' to the oppressed his teacher referred him upon assuming he said 'arms'.[5] In 2018, a young Muslim man suffering from severe illness was reported to Prevent by his physiotherapist for watching Islamic videos. The GP told police, 'The young man cannot walk or feed himself and yet you're asking me if he's a threat or risk'.[6]

As a result of hundreds of similar examples, Prevent is internationally denounced by human rights advocates and academics. But it is important to clarify that the injustice of Prevent is not simply unfair targeting of Muslims based on stereotypes, or its failure to prevent people who have 'actually' been 'radicalised'. When criticisms of Prevent are framed in these ways, they allow government to expand the policy in the name of reforming it. For example, to alleviate Islamophobic bias, we now hear Prevent *also* fights a host of other extremisms. But as we will explore, such adjustments widen, rather than limit, the scope and legitimacy of Prevent policing. This distracts from the real problem: its premise.

Pre-empting violence

Prevent was introduced by the government's 2003 counterterrorism strategy. It aimed to predict who might become a terrorist in the future and intervene in their lives before they do. But the idea that violence can be predicted is unfounded, and when the violence being predicted is terrorism, it is obvious who it will

---

5   https://theguardian.com/uk-news/2021/jun/27/boy-11-referred-to-prevent-for-wanting-to-give-alms-to-the-oppressed (accessed July 2021).

6   Hilary Aked, *False Positives: the Prevent counter-extremism policy in healthcare* (London: Medact, 2020), p. 43.

target: from the get-go, Prevent-funding went to local areas with the biggest proportion of Muslims.[7]

While initially focused on policing people in community and youth groups, under the Coalition government in 2011 Prevent was expanded with the hope that 'there will be no ungoverned spaces'.[8] Then in 2015, the Counterterrorism and Security Act made Prevent law. Since then, approximately 500,000 public sector workers are legally obliged to participate in national security policing and monitoring. So now teachers, doctors, librarians and councillors must watch students, patients and each other for signs they may be violent in the future – 'signs of radicalisation'.

These 'signs' come from a study called the Extreme Risk Guidance 22+ (ERG22+). This is a single study conducted into a small number of people in prison for terrorism-related offenses. It is classified by government so nobody can access it and it has never been peer-reviewed or publicly scrutinised. Hundreds of academics have condemned the government for making this secret study the basis of a public policy; it is extraordinarily undemocratic for a government so adamant that democracy is one of its fundamental values.[9] More importantly, the 'signs' generated from the ERG22+ include the vaguest of behaviours. Every reader will have exhibited most at some point. Take a tally: 'searching for answers to questions about identity, faith and belonging', being 'unwilling or unable to discuss views', 'disas-

---

7   https://theguardian.com/politics/2015/feb/13/prevent-counter-terrorism-support (accessed July 2021); and see Arun Kundnani, *Spooked! How not to prevent violent extremism* (London: Institute of Race Relations, 2009), p. 12.

8   John Holmwood & Therese O'Toole, *Countering Extremism in British Schools?: The Truth about the Birmingham Trojan Horse Affair* (Bristol: Bristol University Press, 2018), p. 51.

9   https://theguardian.com/politics/2016/sep/29/anti-radicalisation-strategy-lacks-evidence-base-in-science (accessed January 2021).

sociating from existing friendship group and becoming involved with a new and different group of friends', 'general changes of mood', 'secretiveness, especially around internet use', 'withdrawn', the list goes on.[10]

Though it seems these risk factors for radicalisation are so general that anyone could be reported to Prevent, research shows that whenever there is broad discretion in a law there is 'the greatest disproportionality and discrimination' because people rely on their own stereotypes – we see this play out in the stop and search rates of Black men, for example.[11] In terms of Prevent, because of two decades of the War on Terror narrative, we live in a context where 'terrorism' is singularly associated with Muslims in the public consciousness. Consequently, the ambiguity of Prevent's 'signs' makes people more, not less, likely to target Muslims.

In private institutions that are not legally bound by Prevent, even vaguer policing is encouraged. In the words of a police officer, everyone 'from the barista in the coffee shop, to staff at major corporations' is told 'to be our eyes and ears when we're not there, and report anything that doesn't feel right.'[12] But what 'doesn't feel right' under norms of secular white supremacy born from colonialism, is Muslimness itself. Think of the 'See it, Say it, Sorted', public-announcement at train stations. Though the tannoy voice makes no hints, we all know which 'sight' needs 'sorting', and which does not.

Accordingly, despite 'radicalisation' never being clearly defined in government documents, the operation of Prevent

---

10   See for example, https://proceduresonline.com/swcpp/torbay/p_sg_ch_ extremism.html (accessed July 2021); and https://dcfp.org.uk/child-abuse/ radicalisation-and-extremism/ (accessed July 2021).

11   Aked, *False Positives*, p. 34.

12   Wendy Fitzgibbon & John Lea, *Privatising Justice: The Security Industry and Crime Control* (London: Pluto, 2020), p. 101.

shows it is broadly understood as a process which transforms 'normal' Muslims, into terrorists. This criminalises all Muslims because the more Muslim you appear to be, in dress, language, action or anything else, the more prone to violence you are assumed to be and the more closely you will be watched. As Moazzam Begg reflected to me, 'in my very first interrogation at Kandahar [US military interrogation centre in Afghanistan] they asked me if someone was pious – did he pray five times a day? They regard piety, prayer, as a marker for being an extremist, or terrorist. Now you can trace that from Kandahar to the Prevent programme'. Racism is not simply an element of Prevent to be surgically removed: it is its basis.

The impossibility of reform

Yet the government would disagree with my analysis. They have made extensive efforts to show that more and more white non-Muslims are being reported to Prevent, as proof that the policy does not racially discriminate.[13] But this misses the point. In scholar Michelle Alexander's words,

> In the era of colourblindness, it is no longer socially permissible to use race, explicitly, as a justification for discrimination ... so we don't ... we use our criminal justice system to label people of colour 'criminals' and then engage in all the practices we supposedly left behind.[14]

---

13 For example, see https://gov.uk/government/statistics/individuals-referred-to-and-supported-through-the-prevent-programme-april-2019-to-march-2020/ individuals-referred-to-and-supported-through-the-prevent-programme-april-2019-to-march-2020 and accompanying reporting (accessed July 2021).

14 Michelle Alexander, *The New Jim Crow: Mass Incarceration in the Age of Colourblindness* (UK: Penguin, 2019), p. 1.

Government can claim Prevent is colour-blind because it does not specify policing Muslims, but its function depends on an Islamophobic context where 'radicalisation' is associated with us.

Furthermore, when white people are reported to Prevent it is not because they are white, but people racialised as Muslim might be reported irrespective of other factors. Muslimness *is* the 'risk factor' in question. Therefore, recent rebranding of Prevent as a tool to fight far-right extremism 'as well as' Islamist extremism does not address the racism the policy relies on. Instead, it hides it behind the language of 'extremism' which attributes violence to a mindset or ideology. Such character-isation of violence is always reductive, but especially when it comes to racist far-right violence which is a direct outcome of state policies. For instance, writing about the 2019 Christchurch mosque shooting in New Zealand, scholar and activist Tarek Younis argued, 'to truly counter far-right violence, we need to focus more on how ethnonationalism and white supremacist logics have become so normalised, they might even get you elected into political office.'[15]

Indeed, the report into the Christchurch massacre found that the gunman was not radicalised on extreme right-wing sites as many commentators assumed. He was simply an avid watcher of YouTube. Upon discovering this, New Zealand's Prime Minister Jacinda Arden said she would make this point 'directly to the leadership of YouTube', missing the point that YouTube reflects currents already in society.[16] If Jacinda Arden admitted this, or

15 https://mediadiversified.org/2019/04/01/the-uks-PREVENT-policy-would-not-PREVENT-white-supremacist-attacks-like-christchurch-its-part-of-the-problem/ (accessed March 2021).

16 https://reuters.com/article/newzealand-shooting-idUSKBN28I0DV (accessed July 2021).

Boris Johnson for that matter, the white supremacy their own governments and states are founded upon would be exposed.

Therefore, far from levelling the playing-field for Muslims, marking more people as 'terrorists' simply justifies expansion of policing apparatuses which are already racialised and thus will harm us further. Criminalising racist or Islamophobic individuals through Prevent or hate-crime legislation will never address the underlying cause of such violence because tools of the state cannot, and will not, resist the state.

Increasing vulnerability

Channel is the name of the Home Office's Deradicalisation Programme that people referred to Prevent are required to attend. However, 90% of Prevent referrals never get as far as Channel because most people are instead signposted to mental health services, social care or educational support after a Prevent referral. This means that people are generally referred to Prevent because their vulnerabilities and need for support are criminalised. So although Prevent is referred to as a safeguarding tool, it blurs concern for harm *to* vulnerable people, with approaching them as harmful *themselves* – in turn making them more vulnerable.

For instance, a psychiatrist involved in reporting two schizophrenic Muslim patients with extreme paranoia to Prevent admitted neither were particularly risky and were severely ill, but their ethnicities and faith played a role in the decision to refer them. The psychiatrist explained that the only way to heal such severe paranoia is antipsychotic medication combined with long-term relationships of trust. He acknowledged that, 'there's no doubt us having arranged for a policeman from the Prevent programme to speak to him will have set [his condition] back a few spaces . . . his suspicion of mental health services would have been compounded by our being associated with the police in this way.'[17] A vulnerable patient's care was severely undermined.

In other cases, Prevent referrals have not only increased vulnerabilities but caused them – particularly mental health problems, such as triggering severe OCD.[18] Additionally, Muslims seeking mental health support then face suspicion from therapists which limits their ability to speak freely. In her essay in *Cut From The Same Cloth?* Sophie Williams recounts her therapist immediately alienating her by deciding, 'one measure of the success of our sessions might be that you feel comfortable taking off [your niqab] in public'. This left Sophie feeling, 'it's the first session, and I'm already trying to reassure my therapist that I'm not dangerous'.[19]

Prevent has irreparably damaged Muslims' sense of safety and relationship with public and social services. Far from supporting us, they criminalise us, ensuring we receive inferior levels of care. The cumulative effect of this means people being less likely to seek support out of fear of being made more vulnerable. For instance, Medact reported a case of a Muslim school pupil referred to Prevent for watching videos online. The referral had the knock-on effect of making it difficult for him to get help when he was later diagnosed with a development disorder, because the family could not trust the school enough to share his diagnosis.[20]

---

17   Aked, *False Positives*, p. 40.

18   Ibid., p. 43.

19   Sophie Williams, 'On Therapy' in ed. Sabeena Akhtar, *Cut from the Same Cloth? Muslim women on Life in Britain* (London: Unbound, 2021), p. 46.

20   Aked, *False Positives*, p. 43.

Knowing that a referral could be around any corner based on signs that are simply part of who you are, coerces all Muslims. The National Union of Teachers, and National Union of Students have highlighted how Prevent alienates Muslim students and staff by imposing self-censorship in discussions. They must continuously evaluate how their words and actions may be read through eyes of racialised suspicion. How will it look if I take this book out from the library? If we go to the prayer room in a group might we seem threatening? How will my opinion about foreign policy be scrutinised? What about if I start covering my hair? [21] Having, or not having anything to hide is beside the point; 'Muslimness' makes Muslims vulnerable to suspicion.

The situation is made even more insidious by the fact that by turning everything, including mental, emotional and other vulnerabilities, into 'risk factors', Prevent hides the structural conditions that produce vulnerabilities and instead victim-blames individuals for experiencing them. As Tarek Younis tells me, 'Under capitalism, reducing risk is about maximising efficiency and productivity. So, although cutting public funding technically increases "risk" to people, the government simultaneously individualises responsibility for "resilience", dislocating it from material conditions.'

An example that comes to mind is how the government claimed that risk factors for radicalisation had been exacerbated by the COVID-19 pandemic. They cited these factors as 'lack of opportunity and employment, increased distrust of the government, and increased social isolation'.[22] But the language of individual 'risks' depoliticised issues better termed as 'gov-

---

21   Matthew Guest et al., *Islam and Muslims on UK University Campuses: perceptions and challenges* (Durham: Durham University, 2020).

22   https://rusi.org/commentary/interception-deterring-radicalisation-during-coronavirus-pandemic (accessed March 2021).

ernment unwillingness to provide financial support during pandemic', or 'prioritisation of capital over human life'. However, such framing would threaten to make oppressive socioeconomic conditions visible as causes of harm, so instead the language of 'risk' is used to hide them, and to criminalise the people they harm.

Given all this, Prevent is yet another way people are caught into the tangle of national security. Everybody reported to Prevent remains on a secretive police database for up to seven years, which can lead to future counterterrorism interventions even when cases have been dropped. PreventWatch, a community-led organisation supporting people impacted by Prevent, tell me that referrals can lead to children being assessed by social workers and the subsequent, 'real or perceived threat of child removal'. Some people have also had assets frozen years down the line, or subsequent searches and interrogations.[23] The data retention aspect also raises questions about how people's future prospects may be adversely impacted by Prevent including in schooling and careers.

Punishing dissenters

In 2017, a presentation aimed at helping University staff fulfil their Prevent duty included a list of views to be monitored. These included 'opposition to Prevent' itself, alongside 'vocal support for Palestine' and 'criticism of wars in the Middle East'.[24] Framing these positions as risk factors enabled the government to police opinions running contrary to its agenda. This makes it potentially unlawful to think critically, let alone speak freely

---

23   Ibid.
24   https://middleeasteye.net/news/revealed-uk-universities-told-manage-palestine-activism (accessed March 2021).

or be involved in political activism. For instance, in response to the heightened visibility of Israeli state violence against Palestinians during May–June 2021, millions of people took part in some of the biggest solidarity protests Britain had seen in years. But dozens of school children who showed solidarity through wearing Palestinian flags or posting on social media faced Prevent referrals in school which effectively punished them for taking a political stance against an injustice that millions across the globe were taking at the same time.[25]

Some Prevent risk factors in young people even refer explicitly to 'perceiving religious or racial harassment'.[26] This implies racism and Islamophobia are not actual, but perceived, and makes recognition of them a sign of radicalisation, and protesting them a signal of future terrorism. These factors particularly target Muslims organising and dissenting against the state, imperialism and racism, marking such struggles as dangerous. These efforts to repress anti-racist and anti-imperialist dissent, even in children, can also be traced to the colonial era.

Unlike more explicit counter-insurgency policing that the last chapter covered, Prevent echoes types of legislation that associated particular racialised bodies with particular crimes to justify pre-emptive policing. For instance, in 1871 Britain passed the first of several Criminal Tribes Acts (CTA) which classified 13 million people in India as criminal by birth. Their ancestors were supposedly 'criminal from time immemorial', so they were also 'destined . . . to commit crimes' and have criminal descendants.[27] This allowed Britain to arrest, isolate and divide

---

25 https://middleeasteye.net/opinion/uk-pro-palestine-activists-targeted-in-schools (accessed June 2021).

26 https://rusi.org/commentary/interception-deterring-radicalisation-during-coronavirus-pandemic (accessed March 2021).

27 James Trafford, *The Empire at Home: Internal Colonies and the End of Britain* (London: Pluto, 2020).

communities at will, restricting their movement, and assigning them hard labour. The racialising language used in 1871 could describe how Black and Muslim people are perceived today in Britain: destined to be criminals and terrorists and therefore in need of civilising and intervention.[28]

In fact, British stop and search laws descended from the CTA as a tool to police racialised people 'at home' – especially after anti-racist uprisings in the 1980s. Stop and search also inherited logics from the British Vagrancy Act of 1824 which enabled police to arrest poor and homeless people 'on suspicion of likelihood of committing an offence.'[29] The legacies of both the Vagrancy Act and CTA are that the practice of attributing particular crimes to particular people has been deemed an effective method to allow broad and unjustified policing. Through demonisation of groups of people deemed criminal by nature, we leave white supremacy, police violence and capitalism unaddressed as harbingers of social violence.

Prevent grows out of these projects. By seeking to pre-emptively police the racialised 'crime' of radicalisation, it enables the state to designate political dissent, anti-racist and anti-imperialist resistance and more, as simply traits of a Muslim pre-destined riskiness and extremism.

But the histories Prevent grows out of show us that coercive racialising logics are not limited to any one group of people. They can be applied and re-applied at the state's convenience. Indeed, while Prevent primarily impacts Muslims, it has already been used to police environmental activists and student movements for 'radicalisation' and 'extremism'.[30] It has also been replicated

---

28 Ibid.

29 Fitzgibbon & Lea, *Privatising Justice*, p. 36.

30 https://amnesty.org.uk/press-releases/uk-deeply-concerning-peaceful-climate-activists-were-referred-dubious-anti-terrorism (accessed March 2021).

to police other racialised crimes. For instance, The Knife Crime Prevention Orders of 2019 enable the state to impose curfews, restrictions on movement, and even child removal, on anyone 'police believe is regularly carrying a knife', to pre-empt 'knife violence' in the future – this disproportionately targets Black youth.[31]

Prevent makes policing more pervasive than former stop-and-search powers because it does not rely on police forces alone. Instead, it conscripts all members of society to pre-emptively police – encouraging all of us to look away from the structures and histories that shape the conditions of our society, and instead to focus on characterising racialised people as 'risky'.

Ending the logic, not just the policy

Since 2019, in response to widespread criticism, the government have declared that Prevent will be independently reviewed. But this is just an attempt at re-legitimisation. All suggested reviewers have been far from independent – the latest being William Shawcross, formerly a member of the Henry Jackson Society that lay the intellectual groundwork for Prevent. More importantly, Prevent cannot be improved by reviewal. The government sometimes asks critics what our alternative is, if Prevent is so bad. But that is the wrong question to ask. Prevent's role in society is not worth replacing in any form. Its strategy of guesswork that pre-criminalises people based on racial profiling does nothing to deal with the root conditions that produce violence; it simply masks them. Any valuable roles it does play, such as sign-posting people to well-being services, could be much better done by institutions other than the police. Moreover, a review distracts

31   Trafford, *Empire at Home*, p. 77; and https://gov.uk/government/news/ introduction-of-knife-crime-prevention-orders (accessed February 2021).

us from identifying that Prevent has already been reincarnated as various counter-extremism projects behind the scenes – a more insidious and less visible force than Prevent – as I explore over the next two chapters.

Scrapping Prevent is not enough then. If we wish to resist its surveillance, we must resist its logic which underpins modern policing in its entirety and seeps into the fabric of society, co-opting social support and safeguarding work every day. That means resisting every piece of national security legislation as well as the premise they work from. All policing of racialised people hides and upholds the socioeconomic conditions that produce violence. To reveal these conditions and directly address violence, our resistance to policing cannot be limited to one group of racialised people, nor can it be limited to one nation.

In Tarek Younis' words, 'Prevent is a local form of a global issue'. Indeed, the Prevent policy underpins 'Countering Violent Extremism' (CVE) policies across the world and specifically the USA.[32] Disturbingly, the UK has also directly promoted Prevent to China, a state currently committing genocide against Uighur Muslims in its Xinjiang province where there is some of the most pervasive surveillance in the world.[33] This has been undertaken as a British Aid project to chillingly 'demonstrate the effectiveness' of Prevent.[34]

Freedom of Information requests also found that the government's reason for classifying the ERG22+ that underpins Prevent, include preventing 'production of a competing product

---

32 http://stopcve.com/ (accessed March 2021).
33 https://theguardian.com/world/2021/mar/09/chinas-treatment-of-uighurs-breaches-un-genocide-convention-finds-landmark-report (accessed March 2021).
34 https://devtracker.fcdo.gov.uk/projects/GB-GOV-3-PAP-CNF-002340 (accessed March 2021).

on the market'.[35] So, Prevent is essentially a British export sold to satiate global demand for surveillance technologies. In 2018 alone the UK made £5.2b selling security services.[36] Given this, our resistance to securitisation and surveillance in Britain must, by definition, be anti-imperialist and in solidarity with racialised and oppressed people across the world experiencing the global War on Terror and all other forms of counterterror policing and CVE. The nation cannot be our horizon.

Due to the pervasiveness of surveillance in society, we may find it difficult to imagine life without it, and so we normalise it, perform for it, and shrink our hopes to the size it tells us to. This intentionally limits our capacity to resist it. But things do not have to be this way. I once saw abolitionist scholar Jackie Wang ask an audience to close their eyes and imagine themselves where they feel safest. She then asked, 'how many police officers did you imagine?' I might add to her question, 'were you spotting signs of radicalisation in the people around you?'

We must establish a consensus that recognises policing in its modern guises is rooted in colonialism and therefore racial violence. Not only does policing not address the root causes of violence, it exacerbates them and deliberately punishes those who seek to resist or expose them. Public sector workers and others given Prevent training can resist implementing it, and we, as people, can collectively resist and transform the conditions that generate and lead people to perpetrate violence. We must do away with Prevent, yes, but to do so, we must build a world on justice and care.

---

35   https://cage.ngo/british-government-uses-failed-PREVENT-as-a-bargaining-tool-in-brexit (accessed March 2021).
36   Department for International Trade, Security Export Strategy: Growing UK exports for global security, (London: UK Government, 2019).

Chapter 5

Whose parallel lives? Which British values?

On 7 July 2001, two months before 9/11 and exactly four years before 7/7, an anti-Nazi demonstration was organised in Bradford, West Yorkshire, to resist the fascist group, the National Front (NF). The NF were expected after marching in nearby Oldham and Burnley that summer, where they had attacked Asian people's homes and businesses. Though the NF were eventually banned from marching in Bradford, a combination of racism and heightened police presence turned that night into 'the worst rioting on mainland Britain in two decades',[1] solidifying the image of Muslims in Britain as angry, violent, brown men.

However, that image had begun to form a decade before when Bradford made global headlines during the so-called Satanic Verses controversy. Here, photographs of Pakistani men setting fire to Salman Rushdie's book, *The Satanic Verses*, were shown in newspapers and on TV screens around the world in 1989, portraying a group of zealous, irrational, Others. But when I look at those photos, I see people like my granddad, who were urged by Britain to migrate from Pakistan to fill labour shortages in Bradford's textile factories in the 1960s. By the 1980s, dein-

1   https://yorkshirepost.co.uk/heritage-and-retro/heritage/20-years-what-did-we-learn-bradford-riots-3072638 (accessed January 2021).

dustrialisation and recession saw those same factories close, leaving Bradford's Pakistani population with some of the highest unemployment and poverty levels in the UK, and the lowest educational qualifications.[2]

The photographs of the 1989 protest, therefore, show an exploited and racially oppressed working class expressing anger and the pain of erasure, sparked by a book portraying their Prophet disrespectfully. But this context is rarely included in the mainstream story about the controversy. Instead, the protest is seen as the moment 'fundamentalist' Muslims reared their heads in Britain. Some historians have suggested that this is because, 'there were no "British Muslims" before this moment of "visibilisation"', which turned a group seen as 'Commonwealth immigrants', or 'black', or 'Pakistani', into being recognised as 'Muslim'.[3]

A decade later, on the eve of the 7 July 2001 riots in response to the NF, poverty levels had rocketed further, and Bradford ranked as the fifth most unequal district for ethnic minorities in terms of education, employment, health and housing.[4] Although the NF were banned from marching on that day, they still turned up, and a huge police presence accompanied them. Instead of protecting the local community, police attacked Asian youth who had turned out in self-defence. Their resistance to police brutality was called 'senseless violence' by the media, but as Martin Luther King reminded us, 'riots are the language of the unheard'. What did it feel like to be jobless, ghettoised by racism,

2 Tariq Modood, 'Muslims, race and equality in Britain: Some post-Rushdie affair reflections', *Third Text*, Vol. 4:11, 1990, 127–34, p. 127.

3 https://sites.cardiff.ac.uk/islamukcentre/2019/02/13/michael-munnik-salman-rushdie-and-the-sudden-visibilisation-of-british-muslims/ (accessed January 2021).

4 Nissa Finney and Kitty Lymperopoulou et al, Local Ethnic Inequalities . . . in Education, Employment, Health and Housing . . . 2001–2011 (London: Runnymede, 2014).

left to the poorest housing, education and jobs, and then when attacked by fascists who hounded your parents for decades, left to find that the people the state said would protect you, kettled and attacked you with batons?

Such questions were not asked by the government. Instead, the Cantle report, which looked into the riots, declared them to have been caused by Muslims living 'parallel lives' that 'do not seem to touch at any point' with the 'rest of society'.[5] In this victim-blaming account, Community Cohesion and Integration were introduced as solutions to social violence, leaving the role of racist policing and contexts of state-sanctioned poverty and racism unchallenged.

Since then, the dominant image of Muslims in the UK has been a reductive and exclusive one of working-class, under-educated, over-angry Asian men. Their violence then, as now, is imagined as the result of self-imposed segregation that allows 'Muslim culture', religion and ideology to flourish in so-called separatist bubbles. Over the years, this 'parallel lives' narrative has been used to justify invasive policing of areas with large Muslim populations, not only through national security and Prevent, but Integration and Community Cohesion strategies, as well as the British Values Counter-Extremism agenda.

'Outside' the nation

One of the most crucial invocations of the 'parallel lives' analysis came about when 52 people were killed in the 7/7 bombings in London in 2005. Three of the perpetrators grew up where I did, down the road from Bradford, in Leeds. In the public imagination this was enough of an explanation for their violence. Much

---

5   Ted Cantle, Community Cohesion: A report of the independent review team (London: Home Office, 2001), p. 9.

like the riots, 7/7 was also presumed to be an outcome of Muslim men growing up in their parallel Muslim world. Politicians and journalists even referred to the men as 'British-born', implying that Britain was only their birthplace, but that they had been raised in enclaves that exist at odds with the space and time of Britain – making their motivations essentially foreign. Such sentiments were widespread, despite the men stating that their actions were in retaliation to British foreign policy, 'until you stop the bombing, gassing, imprisonment and torture of my people, we will not stop this fight . . .'[6]

Just as the US depoliticised the causes of 9/11, the UK used Cantle's thesis to deflect from their foreign policy, and from the failure of the security services to stop the attack, despite having investigated the men previously.[7] Instead, by invoking the segregation of Muslim communities as the cause of 7/7, the solution to violence was presented as more intervention in Muslim lives and the bombings were used to condemn previous multiculturalism policies for supposedly allowing Muslim culture to flourish and nurture terrorists.

In these leaps of logic, 'culture' was presented as distinct from 'race', but it rearticulated it because culture was discussed and imagined as an internal essence Muslims carry and inherit, that inherently clashes with the West and makes us violent. Therefore, despite Muslims identifying with many different cultures, and culture itself including shifting sets of norms, the way the term 'Muslim culture' is invoked in the parallel lives analysis disguised the racism of its application.

Districts with large Muslim populations, like Bradford, Birmingham, Luton and East London, have not only been systematically targeted by Prevent, but due to parallel lives nar-

---

6   http://news.bbc.co.uk/1/hi/uk/4206800.stm (accessed February 2021).

7   https://theguardian.com/uk/2007/apr/30/july7.terrorism (accessed 16 July 2021).

ratives they are frequently constructed as cultural abnormalities or even 'no-go zones', in a wider land of rolling hills and peaceful tea drinkers. For example, in 2018, the *Times* ran an article by Rod Liddle, who wrote he did not mind if 'British Islamists blow themselves up' as long as it is 'somewhere a decent distance from where the rest of us live. Tower Hamlets, for example.'[8] His suggestion implied that the East London borough of Tower Hamlets is 'foreign' and external to Britain due to contamination by its Muslim population.

While Liddle can be dismissed as tirelessly racist, his sentiment is echoed in popular culture with TV documentaries like 'Make Bradford British', or 'The Great British School Swap' exploring how cities lose their 'Britishness' because of Muslim presence. Such portrayal assumes there is a 'true Britishness' beyond the reality of everyday experiences, tapping into a racial nostalgia of a white Britain detached from the racial exploitation and extermination it is built upon. These depictions mainstream the assumption of the Cantle report: that state intervention is required to create social cohesion wherever Muslims are found.

This has made areas with high Muslim population density incredibly vulnerable to invasive policing. In 2008, for example, 200 CCTV cameras were installed in the Sparkbrook and Washwood Heath Muslim-majority areas of Birmingham. They monitored number plates of cars entering and leaving the areas and stored the data for two years. This £3m project was funded by a Home Office scheme for initiatives to 'deter or prevent terrorism'.[9] Clearly, it was assumed that spying on the movements of people in Muslim-majority areas was a legitimate way of

---

8   https://twitter.com/azadaliCCM/status/1054141206182182912?s=20   (accessed January 2021).

9   https://theguardian.com/uk/2010/jun/17/birmingham-stops-spy-cameras-project (accessed March 2021).

fighting terrorism, because the existence of Muslimness without regulation poses an inherent threat. This extends War on Terror rationale, that claims hotbeds of terrorism exist across the world, requiring monitoring and occupation, to British cities themselves.

British values

In 2014, six years after the CCTV surveillance of Birmingham, national newspapers claimed the city was facing a 'separatist plot' by 'conservative and hard-line men' of Pakistani heritage to 'Islamicise' schools.[10] The council had received a photocopy of what appeared to be correspondence between Muslims conspiring to take over schools, titled Operation Trojan Horse. When the letter was leaked to media, it was quickly discredited as a hoax, but journalists still scrambled for racist headlines and it prompted government enquiries, school inspections and court hearings because the notion of 'Islamising' was linked directly to concerns of radicalisation.[11]

Though eventually the court case claiming that students were being radicalised was entirely dropped, by that time the media narrative was established. Teachers and parents caught in the affair never got a chance to clear their names even though the spectacle turned one of the most improving schools in England, serving one of the most disadvantaged constituencies, into a 'failing' school that lost its leading teachers. The pupils whose futures were sacrificed to the appetite of racist journalists and politicians were nobody's concern. Instead, despite never existing, the 'Trojan Horse Affair' was used to reinforce the trope of fanatic Muslim Pakistani men. Further, it prompted another

10 Holmwood, *Countering Extremism*, p. 2.
11 Ibid.

bout of concern over the so-called failure of integration, prompting another government review.

The new review into social integration was conducted by Dame Louise Casey who identified that the central barrier to an integrated Britain was 'cultural and religious practices in communities that are not only holding some of our citizens back but run contrary to British values and sometimes our laws'.[12] This regurgitated Cantle's thesis, but Casey drew a more explicit connection between cultural and religious Others' segregation, 'lack' of Britishness, and criminality. For instance, she highlighted Blackburn, Birmingham, Burnley and Bradford as areas of high 'Pakistani and Bangladeshi' residential 'segregation' (meaning Muslim by conflation, and to the erasure of other Muslim communities) which she deemed a problem because 'areas with ethnic concentration . . . lead to lower identification with Britain'.[13] No comparable concern was raised about areas with concentrations of white people having lower identification with Britain. So presumably white people are born with Britishness already inside them.

Indeed, British values had been defined that year as 'democracy, rule of law, individual liberty, equality, freedom of speech, and tolerance'.[14] As the next chapter explores, the government define Extremism as 'opposition to' British values, therefore racial Others arguably pose a criminal threat until we learn them. But since the values themselves are racialised as white, we are suspended in a state of eternal suspicion because most of us cannot learn our way out of being racialised without paying a high cost. This exposes Britain's myth of integration. Despite the

---

12   Louise Casey, The Casey Review: A review into opportunity and integration (London: DCLG, 2016), p. 5.

13   Ibid., p. 11–12.

14   Ibid., p. 9.

rhetoric, racial Others cannot be absorbed or accepted into British-ness without destabilising the colonial idea of civilisational superiority that Britain is born from. Therefore, while being commanded to integrate on the one hand, racialised people are deliberately excluded from the nation on the other.

Integrating to regulate

The 2016 Casey Review also strengthened the connection between Integration and Counter-Extremism that had been evoked since 7/7. While seemingly distinct, both government strategies rely on the principle that Muslims pose a risk to society if left unregulated, and that only 'British culture', which is imagined as inherently non-violent, can civilise us. But at face value, the Integration Strategy gives no indication that it could be linked to policing or surveillance. For example, integration projects often encompass the likes of afterschool clubs helping children make friends, library coffee mornings combating social isolation, football tournaments that 'build bridges', and gallery exhibitions on 'breaking stereotypes'.[15] But despite claiming to focus on building communities where people socialise, work, learn and live together, as early as 2007, police themselves had asked if, 'in practice, there is any real difference between Prevent and community cohesion'.[16]

Projects that are focused on Muslim women exemplify this overlap best. In 2016, then Prime Minister, David Cameron, announced that Muslim women needed to learn English to

---

15 HM Government, Integrated Communities Strategy Green Paper (London: DCLG, 2018).

16 John Holmwood and Therese O'Toole, *Countering Extremism in British Schools?: The Truth about the Birmingham Trojan Horse Affair* (Bristol: Bristol University Press, 2018), p. 49.

ensure a more integrated society and to counter extremism. He said he wasn't blaming Muslim women; it was the fault of 'the menfolk' in their 'patriarchal societies' who 'haven't wanted them to speak English'.[17] The generalisation that Muslim women don't speak English was tenuous. But for those who don't, government funding for ESOL (English for speakers of other languages) lessons had been cut by £100m over the decade, so blaming Muslim men was a stretch.[18] The word 'menfolk' also deliberately invoked a pre-modern patriarchal culture to solidify the myth of Muslim distinctiveness and barbarism – justifying the need to civilise and integrate us.

Cameron added, 'if you're not able to speak English, not able to integrate . . . you could be more susceptible to the extremist message coming from Daesh'.[19] As linguist, Dr Hanain Brohi, notes, connecting lack of fluency in English to joining Daesh constructed English language as 'impermeable' to ISIS messaging, while 'foreign' languages are made into 'risk factors' for radicalisation.[20] Not only does this echo colonial policies of enforcing English language to civilise, it presents English lessons as a feminist intervention and turns Muslim women into indicators of how integrated Muslims are. Furthermore, through this slippage, integrating us, and deterring us from terrorism become one and the same project.

For example, initial counterterrorism funding was split between the Home Office, which primarily focused on policing

17   https://theguardian.com/politics/2016/jan/18/david-cameron-stigmatising-muslim-women-learn-english-language-policy (accessed February 2021).

18   https://metro.co.uk/2019/06/20/refugees-let-down-after-100000000-cut-from-funding-for-english-lessons-10014841/ (accessed March 2021).

19   https://theguardian.com/politics/2016/jan/18/david-cameron-stigmatising-muslim-women-learn-english-language-policy (accessed March 2021).

20   https://cage.ngo/language-policy-and-its-silent-intimacy-with-counter-extremism (accessed April 2021).

men, and the Department for Communities and Local Government (DCLG), which focused on 'strengthening the role of Muslim women'.[21] In using counterterrorism funding for 'community' projects including women's empowerment programmes,[22] it is clear the government considered them extended strategies of policing. 'Strengthening' Muslim women was essentially viewed as a way to spy on, or discipline Muslim men – an assumption revealing the contradictory way Muslim women are viewed as both in need of strengthening, and strong enough to influence the entire Muslim community. We are not only integration barometers then, but the channel through which Muslim men and children can be deradicalised. The assumption goes that if Muslim women can be civilised, perhaps they can be conscripted to police their communities and civilise their children on behalf of the state.

Indeed, practices of Muslim child-rearing are central concerns to the state. Child Prevent referrals are often made based on constructing Muslim parents as radicalising influences, and as we saw in Chapter 3, counterterror raids see Muslim homes as spaces requiring intervention. In Casey's integration review there was specific emphasis on Muslim women's 'high birthrates' and 'transnational marriages' as 'concerning' barriers to integration.[23] These concerns emerge from historical processes of imagining women as biological and cultural reproducers of nations.[24] Whether or not this should be the case, governments have often promoted motherhood as an act of patriotism when they need population growth, or represented the nation

---

21   Lucinda Maer, *Preventing Violent Extremism* (London: Parliament and Constitution Centre, 2008), p. 6.

22   Naaz Rashid, *Veiled Threats: Representing the Muslim Woman in Public Policy Discourses* (Bristol: University of Bristol Policy Press, 2016).

23   Casey, Casey Review, p. 9.

24   See for example, Nira Yuval-Davis, *Gender and Nation* (UK:SAGE, 1997).

as a woman under attacked to rally men to war. But racialised women are the wrong sort of mothers in Britain; our expected reproduction is threatening to white ethnonationalist identities.

If I, as a Muslim woman, give birth to children with British citizenship, my children disrupt an understanding of Britain as inherently white. The only way for the state to retain control of what Britishness means therefore depends on declaring racialised people as different to 'real' Brits, not because of our birthplace (Britain), but the Otherness that we supposedly inherit and reproduce. Shamima Begum's citizenship revocation was partially an outcome of this. It ensured she could not be understood as a product or reproducer of Britishness. Instead, we are convinced she joined ISIS because of her Muslimness, and not the British contexts she grew up in.

All social issues the state wishes to displace responsibility for are attributed to Muslims in this way. Constructing us as radicalising and barbarising our families, homes and even local areas with a foreignness that destabilises society, justifies overt and covert methods of policing our behaviours, languages, residential patterns and more through the guise of integrating us. Anxieties around integration are therefore really anxieties about how to maintain the lie that there are essential differences between white and non-white Britons. This lie ensures exclusion of the latter and uses racism and Islamophobia to obscure the processes of capitalism and white supremacy that are the factors which actually ensure there can be no social collectivism in Britain.

Whose separatism?

Indeed, aside from problematising and policing Muslims, the language and strategies born from the parallel lives thesis do not even address the problems they claim to. For example, integration projects often target places with high residential segregation, but white separatism, or 'white flight', as it is sometimes known, is rarely ever discussed as the cause of such residential patterns. This is the process of largely white property-owners and businesses leaving inner cities when racialised people move in. It is a pattern traceable to colonial times when, for example, in Sierra Leone, colonial settlers built their residences away from indigenous people from fear of becoming 'too intimate with the natives'.[25] Fears of such intimacy resonate with segments of British society today and are particularly present when Muslims move into an area – one study found that 'homeowners with white British names were more likely to relocate if homeowners with Pakistani and Muslim names moved in within 50 metres'.[26]

Focus on Muslimness as the cause of social division also conceals the way that huge corporations have invaded and divided communities in many cities, buying up communal spaces like cafes, barbers shops or 'ethnic' food markets that were the initial cause of 'white flight'. These are redeveloped into property and services unaffordable to local residents who are forced out by rising rents and usually replaced with whiter, wealthier people. It is worth considering that it is these new residents who live 'parallel lives' in a superimposed landscape of expensive cafes, gyms and refurbished apartments that local people live in the shadows of. This is not a tit-for-tat point. It is precisely through obscuring the role of whiteness and capital in *creating* residential segregation through racism and gentrification that the myth of Muslim Otherness is secured.

25 James Trafford, *The Empire at Home: Internal Colonies and the End of Britain* (London: Pluto, 2020), p. 31.
26 https://theconversation.com/white-british-homeowners-more-likely-to-move-out-if-pakistanis-buy-houses-nearby-114477 (accessed July 2021).

In 2019 I briefly worked on a sports project with Muslim women that was funded by the London Mayor's 'Sport for Integration' strategy in Tower Hamlets. But it was glaringly obvious from the start that playing sports with Muslim women had no bearing on the socioeconomic causes of social dissolution. No matter how good the sessions made participants feel, they were still being pushed out of their homes by corporations aided by the state. This was displacing their social lives and worsening mental and physical health. Effectively, they were being problematised for not engaging with unaffordable spaces dominated by young white professionals, or, for not exposing themselves to their corresponding racism.

Integration projects address none of this. To achieve any real 'cohesion', government money would be better spent on building high-quality, affordable housing, applying rent-controls, and ensuring secure disability and housing benefits so exploited communities can afford to live without fear of losing their homes and social networks to corporate landlords. Moreover, the 'positive local relationships' that the Integration Strategy seeks to produce,[27] can only be developed if racialised people are not policed in continual stop-and-searches for knife crime, on suspicion of radicalisation in every public institution, or by the hostile environment which excludes immigrants at every turn. No matter how well-meaning the people who work on integration projects may be, integration does not address the issues that underpin social dissolution because it does not tackle structural violence; it simply provides another route for the state to blame and regulate racialised people.

At the same time, while exposing the inherent racism of government cohesion strategies it is important that we do not

27   Home Office, Community Cohesion: SEVEN STEPS – A practitioner's toolkit (London: Office of the Deputy Prime Minister, 2005), p. 3.

over-romanticise the sense of community that existed prior to gentrification, or that we suggest that without the presence of the state, mutual relations are inherent and convivial. In fact, despite the flattened imagining of Muslims as a singular 'foreign' entity who live separately from the rest of society, any sense of 'cohesion' even among Muslims in the UK is starkly intercut by class, gender, anti-Black racism, colourism and other power dynamics. In fact, the general conflation of 'Muslim' with Pakistani and Bangladeshi populations over the past decades has largely excluded many Black Muslim communities from being imagined as Muslim, even by Muslims – doubly exacerbating their lack of access to safety and space. It would therefore be disingenuous to imagine that an organic unity exists in absence of the state and capitalism. Instead, social unity is something we must actively work to build through uprooting racial hierarchy and economic exploitation in all their guises – not only when they are upheld by the state. Rather than 'integrated' communities, we require liberated communities which we will only build through a collective struggle that entails intimate processes of accountability with one another, as much as holding the system to account.

Chapter 6

The revolution must be counter-extremist: Co-opting resistance

In the government's 2015 Counter-Extremism Strategy, they defined extremism as 'the vocal or active opposition to our fundamental values, including democracy, the rule of law, individual liberty and the mutual respect and tolerance of different faiths and beliefs.'[1] The state blatantly contradicts all these values through its own actions, but more significantly, because racialised people are imagined to innately lack such values, in practice, countering extremism is just another method of policing and punishing racialised people. Yet it presents a very different face to other surveillance tactics we have encountered so far in this book. In fact, it uses a deliberately more patriotic and liberal-sounding façade, such as the innocuously-titled work stream, 'Building a Stronger Britain Together'. As a result, a web of surveillance has been woven that we do not even recognise as a web. Not only does this threaten the scope and space for activism, but counter-extremism strategies also increasingly masquerade as activism and dissent themselves, co-opting and threatening to undermine our very understanding of resistance.

---

1   Home Office, Counter-Extremism Strategy (London: Home Office, 2015), p. 9.

In 2019 I withdrew from participating in an arts festival where I was due to read poetry because I found it – the Bradford Literature Festival (BLF) – included in a list of organisations funded by the main programme of the 2015 Counter-Extremism Strategy, Building a Stronger Britain Together (BSBT). BSBT is described as being, 'for groups involved in counter-extremism projects in their communities'.[2] When I asked BLF's founder, a Muslim woman, why the festival was listed in this way, she explained how the money had been used to deliver workshops for local women to improve their literacy skills. While she accepted that this should not be considered a 'counter-extremism project', she told me that money in the arts was scarce.

True as this may be, it does not alter the alarming fact that taking this money not only reinforced the imagined connection between Muslim women's literacy, integration and acts of violence. BLF would also have to report back to BSBT on how their project met its funding criteria of countering extremism. BSBT's effectiveness is evaluated based on measures such as, 'fewer people holding attitudes, beliefs and feelings that oppose shared values', or an 'increase in sense of belonging'.[3] Would it therefore be reasonable for a literary workshop facilitator to consider a quiet woman who is alienated by Islamophobia, as not exhibiting a 'sense of belonging', and thus extremist? Or to consider a participant's angry rant against government policy as 'opposition to shared values'?

I withdrew from the festival because BLF took no action to return or denounce the BSBT funding at the time. I felt it undermined a duty of trust to Bradford's long-surveilled Muslim

2   https://gov.uk/guidance/building-a-stronger-britain-together   (accessed   July 2021).

3   Home Office, Building a Stronger Britain Together Report 2019 findings (London: Home Office, 2019), p. 5.

community because accepting the funding conceded that any work engaging Muslims should approach us as subjects at risk of future terrorism. I got BLF's agreement before publicising my statement of withdrawal where I wrote, 'The government's Counter Extremism (CE) strategy relies on the premise that Muslims are predisposed to violence and therefore require monitoring and surveillance . . . Taking CE funding gives CE credibility even if there is hope to use the funding in other/unanticipated ways – especially when taken by Muslim organisations/ Muslim-led organisations.'[4] This sparked others to withdraw alongside me, including Lola Olufemi, Audrey Sebatindira, Malia Bouattia, Paula Akpan, Siana Bangura, Hussein Kesvani, Lowkey and more. Some of us coordinated with local community groups, trade unionists and students to organise an alternative festival where we shared our work and created space for planning local resistance to surveillance.

National media were quick to cover these events, but their focus swiftly moved away from CE and BSBT, to the 'extremity' of our response. Media outlets pitted me against Muslims and journalists of colour whose positionalities and opposition to my stance, effectively highlighted mine as an extreme outlier.[5] Most interestingly, a 50-page report non-ironically subtitled, 'How Muslims are intimidated and marginalised for supporting counter-extremism initiatives' was published by the right-wing think tank, Civitas. They described our withdrawal as evidence of 'a concerning state of affairs over counter-extremism efforts

4   https://thebrownhijabi.com/2019/07/01/statement-on-building-a-stronger-britain-together-counter-extremism-fund-and-withdrawal-from-bradford-literature-festival-full-text/ (accessed February 2021).

5   For example see, https://theguardian.com/commentisfree/2019/jun/24/bradford-literary-festival-counter-extremism-funding-boycott (accessed March 2021); https://bbc.co.uk/programmes/m0006chf; and https://bbc.co.uk/programmes/m00061b3.

in the UK' – implying that we 'intimidated' BLF.[6] Therefore in refusing to normalise the government's CE strategy, we were constructed as extreme, and even, as marginalising Muslims. This report and the media coverage are part of a wider pattern of delegitimising resistance to state violence and racism that this chapter explores.

BSBT have supported 244 organisations with £8.8m to 'tackle extremism' since 2016.[7] This includes theatre ensembles, Barnardo's, youth clubs, interfaith groups, football clubs, asylum seeker support networks, housing associations and even anti-racism charities like Hope Not Hate.[8] The fact that anti-racist organisations and those supporting refugees take CE funding undermines their work. How can they support people oppressed by the Home Office's hostile environment or state violence if they are paid by that state to see such critique as 'un-British' and a sign of potential future violence?

Today, living back in Leeds where I grew up, I have noticed that nearly every local initiative is tangled in the CE web: a youth club seeking participants for an oral history project, the mosque they are situated next to, the community centre two streets away. I wonder what it would be like to be a Muslim teenager growing up here now. What sort of ideas can you develop if everything you interact with is obliged to monitor you from police, to school, to your football club and even anti-racist charities? What analyses do the adults around you encourage when you discuss racism or Islamophobia? What happens if you

---

6   Liam Duffy, *The 'No True Muslim Fallacy': How Muslims are intimidated and marginalised for supporting counter-extremism initiatives* (London: Civitas, 2019), p. 23.

7   https://gov.uk/government/publications/building-a-stronger-britain-together-bsbt-progress-report-2019 (accessed March 2021).

8   See 'BSBT supported groups' at https://gov.uk/guidance/building-a-stronger-britain-together (accessed March 2021).

critique the state? And what space is there to discuss ideas you know are viewed as 'dodgy'? As Arun Kundnani argues, 'The best way of preventing terrorist violence is to widen the range of opinions that can be freely expressed, not restrict it.'[9] And yet the latter is exactly the strategy pursued by the state. This disregards even superficial notions of free speech in specifically racialised ways, and it demonstrates that despite Muslims being characterised as 'opposing' values of democracy, rule of law and tolerance, they rarely apply to us in the first place.

British capitalism, un-British protest

Austerity is partially responsible for the proliferation and normalisation of CE projects. Over a decade of government cuts to local services have left communities willing to accept any funds they can find to launch projects that will improve the lives of neighbours, friends and local youth. The state exploits this desperation of its own making by replacing social funding with money tied to CE, transforming a range of social initiatives into channels of surveillance. It also places responsibility for social well-being onto hundreds of disparate local organisations and mutual aid efforts instead of the state.

At the same time as capitalism's devastation is hidden and preserved by the state, anti-capitalism is portrayed as 'un-British' extremism. In 2020, school guidance was released urging teachers not to use resources with 'extreme political stances', including anti-capitalism. This framed capitalism as a British value, and property as a victim to extremism. Simultaneously, people exploited for capital accumulation, and forced to sell their time to barely cover rising rents and mortgages, become

9 Arun Kundnani, *A Decade Lost: Rethinking Radicalisation and Extremism* (London: Claystone, 2015), p. 6.

potential extremists to be managed. Are they isolated or angry at the government? That's opposition to our shared values! The point is not that such people are 'not extremists' or that capitalism should *not* be a British value, but that counter-extremism is simply a tool to repress whatever threatens the state's interests or threatens to make them visible.

This was made obvious in 2020 when the environmental activist group, Extinction Rebellion (XR), were included on a police list of 'extremist ideologies'.[10] Due to national outrage, police recalled the document, claiming an 'error of judgement' in their inclusion of XR alongside 'neo-Nazi' and 'Islamist' groups. But the problem was not XR's inclusion (they have been complicit with a securitised approach to threat, themselves),[11] it was the fact a list of extremist ideologies compiled by the state exists at all. Why are fossil fuel companies extracting oil in the USA's imperialist War on Terror not deemed extremists? What makes their actions legitimate, but not those who resist them?

The list XR were included in was part of a guide warning that young people involved in non-violent actions such as sit-ins, banner-drops or walk-outs should be monitored. Targeting such actions as extremist criminalises political activism in total – CE masks the state's attempt to make its agenda the only legitimate agenda one can have. Indeed, on the back of XR actions and Black Lives Matter protests in 2020, the government planned sweeping new police powers via the Police, Crime, Sentencing and Courts Bill that was widely opposed throughout 2021. It aims to widen the conditions police can impose on protests to

---

10   https://theguardian.com/environment/2020/jan/13/priti-patel-defends-inclusion-of-extinction-rebellion-on-terror-list (accessed January 2021).

11   James Trafford, *The Empire at Home: Internal Colonies and the End of Britain* (London: Pluto, 2020), p. 140.

prevent 'disruption', undermining the very nature of protests, as they will only be able to take place with state permission.

While such proposals seem extraordinarily draconian, they grow out of the expansion of policing dissent that has been justified by Islamophobia for two decades. If our outrage is only directed at such policing when it impacts white protestors, it is not policing we object to, but policing not being reserved to racialised people.

Co-opting resistance

During the Black Lives Matter revolutionary action of 2020, I received an email from two Muslim women from the UK and Europe. One was introduced as a 'CVE advocate at Kofi Annan Foundation', and they asked me to join them in signing an open letter to condemn the murder of George Floyd and demand 'peacebuilding measures to address structural racism'. I was bewildered that an advocate of CVE (Countering Violent Extremism) could sign this letter without condemning their own foundation which is part of a security industry built on structural racism and policing. Instead, through the letter, they framed CVE as an anti-racist movement. I had witnessed similar rebranding when a think tank had invited me to join their 'Youth CVE Activist Network'. Labels like activism and advocacy rebrand CE surveillance as revolutionary, as opposed to invested in global dynamics of oppression. Such 'woke-washing' is taking hold in Britain too.

In 2018 the Commission for Countering Extremism (CCE) was set up to 'build a movement to defeat extremism'. It portrays itself as independent from the state, going so far as to be featured in a British *Vogue* article in 2019, entitled, 'The Women at the Forefront of the Fight Against Extremism'.[12] This article included Sara Khan, then lead commissioner of CCE, alongside two other Muslim women in the field. In writer, Sumaya Kassim's words, the article portrayed them as 'beleaguered but empowered figures in a "largely male battleground", committed to "keeping us safe".'[13] Framing CE as a form of women's empowerment allowed a 'series of sleek images to casually gloss over the profoundly troubling industry that women are a part of.'

This 'glam-washing', as scholar, Shereen Fernandez termed it, disguised the fact that while Sara Khan tried to position herself as a grassroots activist, her former organisation, Inspire, had close government links, worked on campaigns within the Office for Security and Counter Terrorism, and received Home Office funding.[14] Voicing such facts is often labelled misogynistic, Islamophobic or both. But as Kassim tells me, this is a deliberate strategy. Using Muslim women as the face of Islamophobic industries acts 'as a kind of shield, where instead of focusing on the valid criticism of counter extremist measures, the media and the women who are employed by the state interpret all criticism as bullying'. Security industries clearly benefit from having Muslim women advocates. As a result, CE not only attempts to co-opt activism; some CE initiatives try to co-opt Muslim identities themselves.

Engineering identities

In 2017 I was contacted by a social media platform 'catering to young British Muslims' called This Is Woke (TIW). They asked

---

12   https://vogue.co.uk/news/article/yasmin-green-nikita-malik-sara-khan-counter-extremism (accessed January 2021).

13   https://gal-dem.com/why-is-vogue-glamourising-the-war-on-terror/ (accessed January 2021).

14   https://middleeasteye.net/news/top-anti-extremism-campaigner-linked-uk-covert-propaganda-firm (accessed March 2021).

if we could make a film together – a conversation that quickly turned into a coffee. Soon, though, they told me they couldn't move forward due to a staff member leaving. It was a shame, but I didn't think about it again for two years until in 2019, TIW was exposed as a Home Office project aimed at finding grassroots voices to communicate government-approved messages. Alarmingly, I realised they had probably asked to meet me to assess whether I could be an agreeable mouthpiece.

TIW was created by RICU, the Research, Information and Communications Unit in the Office for Security and Counter Terrorism. One part of RICU's secretive work focuses on contracting public relations companies to find or create 'grassroots' voices to convey messages 'that feed into national counter-extremism policy objectives'.[15] In the case of TIW, it was the invention of Breakthrough Media, a communications company contracted by RICU. This goes beyond all forms of policing and security this book has so far explored because the purpose of paying companies to package government propaganda through grassroots channels is not only to regulate ideas but to shape and change them. In particular, RICU targets Muslims aged 15–39.[16]

Past RICU projects have included 'Help for Syria', where Breakthrough Media supported three charities to run a campaign encouraging British Muslims to help Syrians by donating to government-approved charities. But this was an outcome of unevidenced Islamophobic concerns from the security establishment that British Muslim charities providing relief efforts were actually going to Syria to join IS. The government was keen to only promote providers of aid that they recognised, thus RICU's

---

15   Rachel Briggs & Sebastien Feve, Policy Briefing: Countering the appeal of extremism online (Institute for Strategic Dialogue, 2014), p. 14.

16   https://middleeasteye.net/news/revealed-woke-media-outfit-thats-actually-uk-counterterror-programme (accessed July 2021).

'Help for Syria' project was essentially a propaganda piece to support this policy decision.[17]

Another project is 'Imams Online', a website supposedly developed by Muslim leaders to support implementation of Prevent in mosques and madrassas. The fact that the Home Office pours huge amounts of resources into making its propaganda appear organic, demonstrates that it knows its work is illegitimate. Moreover, RICU is protected by the Official Secrets Act and withheld from parliamentary scrutiny – not very democratic for part of a system that calls opposition to democracy a sign of extremism.

Interestingly, CE propaganda-work is not always about encouraging actions or ideas, it also cultivates political docility. SuperSisters is the best example of this. It is a 'lifestyle' platform for Muslim girls built by J-Go Media who were funded by BSBT. When asked by journalists, J-Go declined to comment on whether they also worked with RICU. Nonetheless, the SuperSisters social media platform aims to inspire a teenage-Muslim-girl lifestyle that is state-approved and apolitical. Their Instagram page (@supersistersmag) is full of quotes from Lady Gaga to Amy Schumer, and videos of young women discussing sport, friendship and 'positivity' to counter 'hate'. Their singular 'Islamophobia Awareness Month' post in 2020 focused on 'ways Muslim women contribute to UK society . . . through community projects, [being] CEOs of their own businesses, spreading a positive message or breaking barriers'.[18] Such depoliticised and neoliberal measures of 'success' obscure structural violence and

17   Ben Hayes & Asim Qureshi, *We Are Completely Independent, The Home Office, Breakthrough Media and the PREVENT Counter Narrative Industry* (London: CAGE, 2016), p. 21–2.

18   https://instagram.com/p/CIA4ggnFzDO/?utm_source=ig_web_copy_link (accessed April 2021).

the causes of Islamophobia, aiming to cultivate an uncritical understanding of the world among young Muslims.

At first glance, the coercion of CE operations like SuperSisters is not as obvious as that of citizenship removal, home raids or border stops. But in some ways, it is more sinister, because CE attempts to engineer who we are and how we think. The natural conclusion of such engineering and indoctrination can be seen in the extremely secretive detention of over a million Uighur Muslims by the Chinese state in so-called 're-education camps'. Detainees have reported that on top of systematic physical and sexual abuse and torture,[19] they are forced to denounce Islam, have abortions, pledge allegiance to China, learn a sanitised national history and are watched 24/7 for signs they may be attempting to pray.[20] Connecting the promotion of Instagram propaganda to 're-education' camps in genocidal conditions may seem dramatic, but these projects are within the same continuum of socially engineering Muslim identities to become nationalistic and depoliticised, and they are rooted in the same logic of coercion and surveillance. In fact, in the words of the Chinese foreign ministry itself, 'practices in China are no different from those in the UK, France and the US. They are all the active efforts we have made to prevent terrorism and eliminate extremism…'[21]

Consequently, we must urgently recognise that while more visible arms of the national security system are being contested, CE has seeped into the norms of society so that by the time we agree on repealing policies like Prevent, CE will have taken its

19   https://bbc.co.uk/news/world-asia-china-55794071 (accessed March 2021).

20   https://theguardian.com/world/2021/jan/12/uighur-xinjiang-re-education-camp-china-gulbahar-haitiwaji (accessed July 2021).

21   https://fmprc.gov.cn/mfa_eng/xwfw_665399/s2510_665401/t1606828.shtml (accessed March 2021).

place already. Its normalisation coerces our imaginations so we begin to believe there is no problem that cannot be better solved by policing and profit-making. It is more sinister that CE has made policing a part of mundane everyday life through exploiting austerity, co-opting the language of activism, and trying to engineer Muslim identities, than the fact it represses activists. The latter is toxic, but the former lays the groundwork for a future in which there *are* no activists.

Only hateful people and crimes of hate

Alongside their *Vogue* coverage in 2019 the CCE released a report focused on a 'new' category of extremist behaviour they called 'hateful extremism'.[22] Government bodies discovering new forms of extremism is reminiscent of the enlightenment thinkers who 'discovered' racial hierarchies. Then, as now, the aim of such pseudoscientific discovery is the justification of violence. Where enlightenment thinkers enabled colonisation and slavery, the CCE and others enable coercion. Indeed, in their 2021 report, co-written by Sara Khan and former head of Counter-Terrorism, Mark Rowley, they called for more legislation to criminalise 'hateful extremism' which they defined as,

activity or materials directed at an out-group who are perceived as a threat to an in-group motivated by or intending to advance a political, religious or racial supremacist ideology: a) To create a climate conducive to hate crime, terrorism or other violence, or b) Attempt to erode or destroy the fundamental rights and freedoms of our democratic society.[23]

22　Commission for Countering Extremism, Challenging Hateful Extremism (London: CCE, 2019), p. 25.
23　Commission for Countering Extremism, Operating with Impunity: Hateful extremism: The need for a legal framework (London: CCE, 2021), p. 6.

Ironically, this describes the basis of British nationhood which marks racialised Others as a threatening 'out-group' to an 'in-group' defined as white, to uphold white supremacy. But the 124-page report was more concerned with criminalising ideas, than addressing structural causes of harm. The language of 'hateful extremism', like the language of 'cultural extremism' enables this by depoliticising everything to the point that mentioning white supremacy, colonialism or capitalism itself would be deemed 'hateful'.

This is part of the reason I have not been able to call on a wealth of examples of groups resisting Islamophobia in this book. Not because there is not resistance, but because recognisable forms of organised resistance to Islamophobia are effectively criminalised unless they limit their concerns to 'hate crimes' and see legislation as the solution. But addressing securitisation, policing and imperialism as the source of Islamophobia frames you as an extremist. Take the NGO, CAGE, for example. They are one of the only Muslim-led organisations in the UK who actively work against the violence of counterterror legislation and War on Terror abuses, and they are widely derided as an 'Islamist front', full of 'terrorist-sympathisers'. Even Muslims who support their work have the affiliation weaponised against them, as I explore in Chapter 10. Such repression of Muslim resistance to Islamophobia is even more blatant elsewhere. In 2020, the French government sent letters of dissolution to Muslim-run organisations they called 'separatist', including the largest NGO tackling Islamophobia, Collective Against Islamophobia in France (CCIF), who were forced to relocate to Belgium. Civil organisations in Denmark and Austria have been shut down on a similar basis.

'Counter-extremism' is therefore a euphemism to repress and obscure all structural violence to the extent that naming it counts as 'extremism' itself. This helps solidify a structure of policing that stretches from overt militaristic violence overseas, to psychological indoctrination at home. As a result, the public sector, civic life, arts, charities, NGOs, even grassroots spaces, social media platforms and the meaning of anti-racism have been swallowed by policing agendas that use propaganda and co-option to depoliticise us. Although this has happened in the name of countering a Muslim threat, its violence will never be limited to Muslims, as recent expansions to policing powers have shown.

We cannot wait for CE to be completely normalised before we resist it. We must recognise that seemingly small concessions such as accepting BSBT funding, accepting CVE as 'activism', or ignoring CE because it only seems to relate to Muslims, sacrifices the ability of everyone harmed by the state to name and protest the ways it harms us. This means sacrificing our ability to shape our own futures, and to live free from violence. As Chinese detention of Uighur Muslims show, the logic of CE ultimately requires the complete elimination of not only dissent, but difference. Any form of non-compliance becomes punishable. Conceding to this not only concedes to state hegemony and structural oppression, but to a compromised version of life, and of Islam, which I now turn to.

Chapter 7

Compromising Islam for patriotism: A secular state? A Western Islam?

What happens when I come to realise the way I speak is more a result of the War on Terror than the Quran? – Yassir Morsi[1]

One of the most profound but underacknowledged impacts of Islamophobia is on Muslims' own relationships to Islam. While we must understand Islamophobia as a tool of coloniality, the impact of its race-making, counterinsurgency and co-option on Muslims *as* Muslim must be accounted for too. These processes impact everyday Muslims' ability to practice and narrate Islam, to participate in Islamic institutions, critique other Muslims and even impart knowledge. Therefore, our analysis of Muslims as a racialised category comprising Muslims and those perceived to be, must not overlook the fact that racialisation of Islam has spiritual repercussions.

Anti-racism that shows solidarity with Muslims as racialised subjects, but still sees Islam itself as embarrassingly unmodern,

---

1 Yassir Morsi, *Radical Skin/Moderate Masks: De-radicalising the Muslim and Racism in Post-racial Societies* (Maryland: Rowman & Littlefield, 2017), p. 194.

remains counter-intuitively invested in racial logics that construct Islam as backwards, barbaric and unenlightened. In my experience of being invited to discuss Islamophobia in anti-racist spaces, conversations about Muslims as a racialised group are welcomed; but when I ask for space to pray, or otherwise demonstrate adherence to Islam, I am often met with uneasiness. This is not simply a 'secular' discomfort with public displays of religion. It stems from the construction of Islam itself as Other. If our anti-racism does not account for this and the colonial foundation of secularism, how anti-racist is it really?

As mentioned in Chapter 1, secularism emerged as a European political project to limit the institutional power of the Church. It attempted to reconstitute Christianity as merely 'belief' limited to private conscience,[2] but simultaneously, states used Christian missionaries to advance their colonial interests abroad, constructing Christianity as part of Europe's racial superiority *alongside* its secularism.[3] As a result, only European Christianity was considered able to modernise to become secularism, whereas 'religion' was invented as a category that classified the underdevelopment of racial Others.[4] Consequently, secularism does not represent neutrality, it upholds racial hierarchy.

Scholar and researcher, Suhraiya Jivraj, shared a recent example of how this manifests in everyday life. She recounted to me,

> a case was brought by an Italian school parent to the European
> Court of Human Rights about there being a crucifix in the

---

2   Saba Mahmood, *Religious Difference in a Secular Age: A Minority Report* (Princeton: Princeton University Press, 2015); and Talal Asad, *Formations of the Secular: Christianity, Islam, Modernity (Cultural Memory in the Present)* (Stanford: Stanford University Press, 2003).

3   Mahmood, *Religious Difference*, p. 34.

4   Ibid.

central hallway of the school. The discussion was about what work the symbol was doing in a secular school environment. The judgement was that ultimately the crucifix was a 'passive symbol' that did not disrupt the secular space. So, you have the 'passive crucifix' and, as other European Court rulings show, the 'active hijab'.

Clearly, secular does not equate to unbiased and taking secularism for granted in anti-racism reproduces racism, especially Islamophobia. It also makes sure the harm of that investment is illegible and thus unacknowledged.

Epistemic racism

Consider a Muslim woman forced to remove her hijab and photographed under Schedule 7. She experiences a racial, sexual and gendered violation, but there is also another dimension. Being coerced to stop practicing a 'religious' action intrudes on your relationship to Allah, but even as that intrusion is made it is disregarded as violent because your reality is not deemed valid. This is a result of what sociologist Ramon Grosfoguel defines as 'epistemic racism'.[5] The process whereby non-Western forms of knowledge are not only deemed inferior, but illegitimate. For example, indigenous forms of historical records, or medicinal and scientific knowledges have been classed as 'magic', 'superstition', 'religion' or 'belief', as compared to Western 'truth' and 'science'. Forced removal of hijab is not deemed truly harmful because of this colonial belief that 'the true, the objective, the real, the rational and even the scientific emerge only with the

5   Ramon Grosfoguel, 'The Structure of knowledge in Westernized Universities: Epistemic Racism/Sexism and the Four Genocides/Epistemicides of the Long 16th Century', *Journal of Contemporary Islamic Thought*, Vol. 23:91, 2018, p. 71–106.

shedding of religious authority'.[6] Subsequently, it is rare to find non-Muslims who are concerned about forced removal of hijabs, hijab and niqab bans, or incarcerated Muslims being prevented from praying in congregation.[7] These acts are not seen as inherently harmful even when *intended* to harm.

Consider, for example, the infamous torture of Muslim prisoners at Abu Ghraib US military detention centre in the early 2000s in Iraq. This was violent not only in the ways the world witnessed through explicit images of torture circulated throughout news media, but also because of the specific degradation intended by stripping Muslim men in front of female prison guards. This was known to be specifically debasing for them on gendered religious grounds but is rarely discussed as gendered abuse. So, at the same time Islam is deemed illegitimate, it is weaponised in ways a secular lens erases even as it enacts.

Most anti-racists do not grapple enough with the fact that secularism entails discrediting most knowledge produced outside of Western European men's academic thought and is therefore an extension of the colonial project. If you finish this book able to articulate Islamophobia as the cultivation of an imagined racial threat that justifies global imperialism and policing, but remain disconcerted that I worship Allah, it is worth considering your continued investment in the construction of European whiteness as the superior, universal end-goal for all. That is not my end-goal, nor can it be the end-goal of anti-racism.

Secular theological interventions

Another of the many ironies of secularism is that while we assume it means separation from religion, it has always been a

---

6 Talal Asad et al, *Is Critique Secular?: Blasphemy, Injury and Free Speech* (New York: Fordham University Press, 2013), p. 11.

7 Raheel Mohammed & Lauren Nickolls, *Time to end the silence: The experience of Muslims in the prison system* (London: Maslaha, 2020).

way for states to construct it. Consider France. French sociologist and feminist, Christine Delphy, writes that French secularism is not just a prohibition against expressing faith in public, but specifically a prohibition against expressing Muslimness.[8] In fact, *laïcité* (French secularism) has never been invoked to prohibit state upkeep of 36,000 churches, or condemn almost half of French children attending religiously-run (mostly Catholic) schools.[9] Nonetheless, in November 2020, the French government gave the French Council of Muslim Faith 15 days to agree to a 'republican charter of principles' to define an 'Islam of France', on grounds that it was currently incompatible with the nation.[10] The charter demanded they agree to supporting *laïcité*; agree that accusations of 'so-called State racism' are 'slander'; and that 'Islam is a religion, not a political movement'.[11] Disturbingly, they announced that conclusions would be drawn about organisations that did not sign the charter.

President Macron described this project as building an 'Islam des Lumieres': an Islam of Light. Presumably this contrasts with the Islam of 'darkness' that Muslims are prone to without European intervention. In this civilising language, only Europe can save Islam from its barbarism, but to become European, Islam must be secularised. Secularising Islam entails privatising it to personal conviction that does not inform political stances, and ensuring it consents to the ultimate authority of the state – so much so that mentioning structural racism is classified as slander. Far from being detached from religion, this exemplifies

---

8   Nawal Mustafa, *Muslim Women don't need saving: Gendered Islamophobia in Europe* (Amsterdam: Transnational Institute, 2020), p. 9.

9   Christine Delphy, *Separate and Dominate: Feminism and Racism after the war on terror* (London: Verso, 2015), p. 10.

10   https://bbc.co.uk/news/world-europe-55001167 (accessed March 2021).

11   https://politico.eu/article/france-political-islam-charter-imams-fight/ (accessed March 2021).

the way secular states continue the colonial project of constructing the very meaning of religion.

Similar efforts have been made in the UK where the necessity of a 'British Islam' has been cited in hundreds of documents, speeches and memos. Such calls assume that Islam as it is currently practiced in Britain is not full of local quirks, but a static foreign import – hence backwards – and it is taken for granted that this is dangerous. Neoconservative think tanks have produced multiple reports suggesting Imams born abroad bring more radical versions of Islam to the UK undermining 'British Islam', and meaning mosques and sites of Islamic instruction require regulation.[12] This justifies further criminalisation of Muslims and allows the state to demand a patriotic, state-sanctioned Islam that compromises the very essence of Islam as a borderless submission to truth, which entails demanding justice, not adhering to ethnonationalist state agendas.

Nonetheless, this project for a nation-state-sanctioned Islam has been internalised by many Muslims. Some of us repeat it in subtle ways by connecting the 'future of Islam', to Western Muslims and therefore accepting the pathological barbarism of the 'Muslim world'.[13] Others fall into the trap of using the language of 'British Islam' to disparage immigrant Muslim communities. Another example is apparent in the way the British Islam Conference run by New Horizons describe their work as making the case for democracy, free speech, individual liberty and human rights, 'from within the Islamic tradition'.[14] If, as this book has shown, such liberal values are the vocabulary of colonialism, why make this case? Their work repeats the assumption

---

12   Denis MacEoin, *The hijacking of British Islam: How extremist literature is subverting mosques in the UK* (London: Policy Exchange, 2007).

13   Morsi, *Radical Skins*, p. 115.

14   http://nhorizons.org/about (accessed March 2021).

that Muslims' problems can only be resolved by mimicking coloniality, rather than resisting and scrutinising the racism of the
contexts and states we live in.

Some Muslims go even further. Qari Asim, senior Imam
at Makkah Mosque in Leeds, not far from where I live, works
directly with the state to produce an Islam compatible with its
agenda. He is the senior editor for Imams Online, the counter-
extremism initiative mentioned in the last chapter. He is also
Chair of the Mosques and Imams National Advisory Board –
created by the Home Office's Preventing Extremism Together
taskforce in 2005 – and the government's advisor on defining
Islamophobia. Makkah Mosque has won the 'UK Model Mosque
Award', and in 2020 Qari Asim received an MBE (Most Excellent
Order of the British Empire). He provides a clear example that
the acceptable version of Islam is one that promotes surveillance
and not only avoids but deters criticism of state violence. In
Yassir Morsi's words, this is the project of 'socially engineer[ing]
the Muslim community to fit into the Western state's culture of
forgetting colonialism'.[15]

This has grave consequences for Muslims. How can we trust
our scholars and Imams if they are employed by the Home Office
that terrorises us? How do we know they are not teaching a
politically-compromised version of Islam to allow states around
the world to avoid accountability – as we see in repressive states
across the so-called 'Muslim world'? Are we being indoctrinated
to accept conditions Allah has commanded us to resist? And
how do we scrutinise these dynamics when it is wrongly taken
for granted that undergoing classical Islamic training amounts
to the most ethical behaviour? Far from mosques preaching
extremism, they are now more likely to preach political apathy.

---

15 Morsi, *Radical Skins*, p. 56.

Imam Shakeel of Lewisham Islamic Centre in London told me of the pressures he faces. He is an Imam who has been smeared by media and state as an 'extremist' because of his geopolitical stances and refusal to work with Prevent despite funding offers.

Sometimes I feel the wider Muslim community do not really understand. When you are speaking on the minbar, giving a reminder, you're trying to be relaxed but you're thinking about every statement in the back of your mind. If you use the word 'jihad', the word 'struggle', or you mention Palestine, how might you be perceived? But at the same time, you think, 'I cannot stop talking about my principles and values'. As Muslims we must speak out against oppression wherever it is because it is injustice. But the pressure is there. Then you have local relationships with community groups and others where you're trying to balance how they will deem you saying certain things that are simply part of your religion.

He also explained that the pressure to regurgitate a politically apathetic Islam can create further grievances.

Sometimes a youngster comes into the mosque angry with me. They see me as conforming to the state's agenda because maybe I'm not addressing the issues they want. I have to understand that they feel no one is addressing Palestine, or Yemen, or the Uighur genocide. I have to listen and say, 'I understand, and we will work out how to address it', not say, 'look, don't talk about this'. Even if I disagree, brushing these things away won't resolve them.

Imam Shakeel's insight on this is valuable as he is an expert in de-escalating violence, having spent years dealing with conflict between local gang members, opening communication and reducing vulnerabilities to harm. 'Every youngster, Muslim or not, needs engagement, attention, guidance and support. Rather than arresting and punishing and targeting them, people need love and engagement.' His approach to communal safety seems far more holistic than the state's repression, yet he is labelled the extremist.

Hijacking interpretations?

Efforts to co-opt Muslim identities and Islam have been part of the War on Terror since its inception. RAND is a global policy think tank funded by the US government that focuses on analysis for the military. In 2007 they published a report titled, 'Building Moderate Muslim Networks'.[16] The first paragraph stated, 'radical and dogmatic interpretations of Islam have gained ground in many Muslim societies . . . [they] have intimidated or silenced moderate and liberal Muslims, who espouse the key principles of democratic culture . . . [they] may need external assistance to build [their networks].'

The classification of Muslims as either moderate and liberal, or radical and undemocratic was asserted as fact, and introduced with intent to support the former. The report stated that such support would further the USA's overall goals by engineering a group of Muslims who condone US imperialism. However, they couched this as a benevolent desire to create, 'liberal groups to retrieve Islam from the hijackers of the religion'. Such rhetoric is not reserved to military think tanks. The idea that there is a 'true Islam' which Muslims who perpetrate acts of violence have hijacked, is popular outside policy-making circles, too. Many

---

16   https://rand.org/pubs/research_briefs/RB9251.html (accessed November 2020).

people say this to show sympathy for Muslims by stating it is only a minority who are violent. However, as Kundnani argues, this approach still places the origins of terrorism 'in the content of an ideology that is rooted in an alien culture'.[17] As a result, it still sustains Islamophobia because it accepts that *any* Muslim could be one of the violent ones, subsequently *all* require criminalisation, or, in RAND's case, military intervention.

Moreover, in all cases, violence perpetrated by Muslims is seen to stem from 'Islamic ideology'. Throughout this book, I have asked us to consider how this understanding obscures political contexts, but additionally, let's consider how this constructs Islam. Anthropologist of religion, Talal Asad, explains that such vague terms as 'Islamic ideology' contradictorily assume the Quran has the power to bring about particular beliefs in Muslim readers that compel them to violence; while at the same time assuming violence is the result of readers having the power to falsely interpret the Quran in violent ways.[18] As a result, 'Islamic ideology' and 'religious motivation' are slippery concepts. Asad asks, does an action count as religiously motivated because it is explained by religious discourse, or does it have to be sincerely religious, and how can anyone tell, let alone a secular legal system? In other words, how do we 'distinguish between the religious and the secular'?[19]

Despite such incoherence, discussions about Islamic ideology as the cause of violence often pressurise Muslims to prove that the 'true' Islam is aligned with the values we are attacked for not possessing. For years of my childhood, I remember the slogan 'Islam means peace' being used to articulate that the true Islam

---

17 Arun Kundnani, *The Muslims Are Coming!: Islamophobia, extremism, and the domestic war on terror* (London: Verso, 2015), p. 67.

18 Asad, *Formations of the Secular*, p. 11.

19 Ibid.

is peaceful. But this ironically demonstrated to me that Islam could only be understood in relation to the violence imagined as its defining feature. Islam does not mean peace; it means submission. Specifically, submission to Allah's will. But how convenient that Islam was likened to peace, rather than adherence to a Divine authority who has made seeking justice against oppression incumbent upon us?

By imposing meanings onto Islam while not deeming it a genuine form of knowledge or lived reality, Islamic traditions have been concealed. For example, RAND stated that Sufis are 'natural allies of the West' against 'Salafis and Wahhabis', but mere decades ago Sufi orders posed some of the greatest resistance to Western colonialism, including through militarised resistance. Take the Sanussi order in Libya who fought against Italian colonisers, or the Qadiriyya movement who resisted the French in Algeria in the 1800s.[20] Now, however, 'Sufism' is imagined as apolitical and often reduced to Rumi quotes stripped of their Islam. In 2006 the British government even promoted formation of the Sufi Muslim Council which received over £300,000 of Prevent funding and claimed, 'the Prime Minister and others have . . . rightly called for moderate Muslims to stand up and be counted'.[21]

Clearly, the effort to co-opt Islam for state agendas has impacted not only how Muslims experience Islam, but our knowledge of Islamic history, and ability to narrate it beyond the terms of the War on Terror. But why should we have to

---

20   Fait Muedini, 'Sufism and Anti-Colonial Violent Resistance Movements; The Qadiriyya and Sanussi Orders in Algeria and Libya', *Open Theology*, Vol. 1, 2015, p. 134–45.

21   http://news.bbc.co.uk/1/hi/uk/5193402.stm (accessed February 2021); and see https://hansard.parliament.uk/Lords/2009-12-15/debates/09121577001165/Sufi MuslimCouncil (accessed February 2021).

bottle centuries of history and knowledge into either 'radical', or 'moderate'?

Good Muslim / Bad Muslim

All these narratives burden Muslims to prove we are not 'the bad ones' by showing how charitable, patriotic and invested in representational politics we are. But these performances demand political conformity. To count as 'a good one', you cannot talk about racism, seek more than positive representation, or seek abolition of the capitalist causes that produce the need for charity in the first place.

One of the most recognisable arenas where Muslims are forced to prove we are 'good', is when asked to condemn or explain acts of violence perpetrated by Muslims. This happens in TV debates, conversations in student accommodation, the workplace, or in passing verbal harassment. To ask why it is presumed that you might not condemn such violence, or to refuse to, risks you being deemed a 'bad Muslim'. But as Tarek Younis writes in the anthology, *I Refuse To Condemn*, refusal resists 'our yearning to be seen by Power . . . it is to face the fear of mobilising on our own terms.'[22] Indeed, it is only when we refuse the performance of the 'good Muslim' that we can be Muslims for Allah's sake alone, not the colonial gaze.

In addition, proving yourself to be a 'good Muslim' necessitates accepting that there are 'bad Muslims' somewhere out there, whose violence *is* purely a cultural/ideological result of Muslimness, not a response to political conditions (that could be 'sincerely' Islamically motivated). But if we accept this, we

22   Tarek Younis, 'The duty to see, the yearning to be seen', in ed. Asim Qureshi, *I Refuse to Condemn: Resisting racism in times of national security* (Manchester: Manchester University Press, 2020), p. 77.

implicate all Muslims and maintain that states' techniques of racialised policing are valid. Furthermore, as Muslims, we would be wise to recognise that preferring acceptance through conforming to injustice may have serious spiritual consequences. As US abolitionist, Hoda Katebi, quips, 'if the Prophet Muhammad ﷺ was alive today, don't you think he'd be in prison?'

Given these contexts, Kundnani is right to suggest that the only political act Muslims can perform without suspicion is rejection of their Muslim identity.[23] We see this manifested in the role and reception of 'Ex Muslims', a category of people defined by what they are not. Those like Ayaan Hirsi Ali have made lucrative careers out of positioning their identities around having been Muslim, but now being liberated by the West and able to whistle-blow on the barbarism of Muslims. Such people are valuable because they validate Islamophobic narratives that uphold state-corporate violence, without being able to be levelled with the same critique.

Where is our Islam?

Interventions to repackage Islam ultimately distort our understanding of Islam on our own terms. We are diverted to a host of questions that are not our own, funnelling energy and time into proving that Islam is not inherently misogynistic, proving the greatness of Muslims in the past, the contribution of Islamic scholars to the development of maths and science, or deriding ourselves as blemishes on Islam. But what questions would we pursue if Islam wasn't racialised and securitised in all the ways it is – if we weren't merely 'guarding it against racist attacks'?[24] What claims might we make on the present? What kind of

---

23   Kundnani, *The Muslims Are Coming!*, p. 76.

24   Morsi, *Radical Skins*, p. 165.

Muslims might we be? And what futures might we imagine on our own terms, without caveats?

Secular states' attempts to engineer docile subjects who accept their agendas, are violent in ways that cannot be fully understood through the lens of secularism itself. In fact, secularism refuses to see Muslims as Muslim, but simultaneously polices the parameters of Islam. When anti-racist movements accept such policing, they uphold colonial racialising logics of Islam as barbaric and Europe as superior; and when Muslims internalise these parameters, we submit to a reductive vision of Islam as merely a part of our private identity that stays at home away from 'politics', rather than an impetus to transform our world.

But Islam inherently refuses constraints of personal conviction because it demands that we better the world. We are made responsible and cannot be bystanders. This means Islam threatens the unjust hegemony of nation-states and capital. The fact that states, militaries and security industries invest so much into co-opting Islam implies that Islamic knowledge, submission and a relationship to Allah, are potentially so threatening to the current world-order, that Islam must be entirely reconfigured into the mould of colonial tyranny itself or result in another world altogether.

Chapter 8

Destroying life and hoarding wealth in the name of border security

Shukri Abdi began life in a refugee camp in Kenya due to the conflict in her country, Somalia. She was brought to the UK under a UN scheme for vulnerable refugees in 2017, but on 27 June 2019, aged 12, her body was found in the river Irwell in Greater Manchester. Despite the suspicious circumstances of her death, and months of prior bullying, the inquest ruled her death an accident. In this chapter we turn to the connection between border violence, immigration controls and Islamophobia to consider if the death of a Black Muslim refugee girl can truly be considered an accident under conditions of systemic white supremacy and Islamophobia.

One of the primary justifications for border and immigration controls in Britain – as well as the US, Europe, Australia and elsewhere – is securing the nation against a 'Muslim threat'. The sentiment that unregulated borders enable terrorists to infiltrate 'our lands', has been expressed across the political spectrum, and by journalists who continuously link migration to national security.[1] To give one example, in 2016, Secretary of State for Justice, Michael Gove, claimed freedom of movement would be 'like hanging a sign welcoming terrorists to Europe'.[2] Terrorism therefore joins the list of threats migrants supposedly pose to Western states, including taking 'our' jobs, benefits and women.

Such narratives mean we barely bat an eyelid at the violence borders inflict on migrants and refugees. Moreover, they conceal the fact that Western states are *the* bringers of terror that displace those labelled 'migrants' and 'asylum seekers' in the first place. People seek refuge or movement into Europe because of the impacts of colonialism that stole and disordered natural resources and wealth; imperialism that sets up systems of global debt dependency and creates climate catastrophes; as well as decades of the War on Terror and its subsequent conflicts that have created conditions of violence, destruction, sickness, starvation and misery.

'Immigrant', 'asylum seeker', and 'Muslim' are often conflated in the public imagination, and since Muslims are already pre-criminalised as terrorists, and migrants as trespassers, many people readily accept the state's declaration that most people seeking to enter the UK are 'illegal'. However, it is the law that makes people 'illegal', and in the UK this is on an especially contradictory basis. The UK only accepts asylum claims made inside its borders, forcing most people to enter illegally, to apply to become legal. This process is traumatic and bureaucratic with most applications initially rejected, taking years to repeal. Additionally, many are denied the right to remain because they arrive without official ID documents due to persecution, loss or robbery during perilous journeys, or never having had any in the

---

1   https://unhcr.org/56bb369c9.html (accessed March 2021).

2   https://independent.co.uk/news/uk/politics/eu-referendum-michael-gove-s-full-statement-why-he-backing-brexit-a6886221.html (accessed February 2021).

first place. Being refused asylum leaves people stateless and vulnerable to exploitation because they must hide from the state to avoid deportation.

Indeed, frequent immigration raids target such people, seizing and detaining them for deportation. Raids take place at residential addresses, factories, restaurants and in collaboration with employers from SOAS University, to Byron Burgers.[3] The threat of detention or deportation terrorises vulnerable people, ensuring that undocumented migrants and refugees comply with unjust landlords and with oppressive labour practices imposed by employers in gruelling work such as cleaning, food-picking and packaging. Therefore, what we call 'the border' does not just refer to the edges of the land labelled Britain, it haunts people at work and at home. And passport and immigration-status checks now take place even when you open a bank account, rent a house or apply for jobs.

This agonising system will likely become more punishing. At the time of writing, Home Secretary, Priti Patel, plans to deny the right of asylum to refugees who use illegal routes into the UK in the first place. Without simultaneously opening legal routes this creates an impossible situation in which more life-threatening journeys will be made across the British Channel because safe routes of entry are *made* illegal to those without the right documents. So, although British politicians love to share condolences for drowned refugees, their decisions necessitate those deaths.

In July 2021 when numbers of people crossing the English Channel surpassed the total of all those who crossed in 2020,[4]

---

3   https://theguardian.com/uk-news/2016/jul/28/it-was-a-fake-meeting-byron-hamburgers-staff-on-immigration-raid (accessed March 2021); and https://irr.org.uk/article/soas-occupied-after-cleaners-detained-and-forcibly-removed/   (accessed July 2021).

4   https://news.sky.com/story/mps-back-new-immigration-bill-which-makes-arriving-in-uk-without-permission-a-criminal-offence-12359884 (accessed July 2021).

the Home Office announced it would give France £54m to prevent crossings on their end. In 2020, the government had already deployed a $29m military drone to monitor and intercept migrant boats crossing the English Channel.[5] Such spending and use of expensive military technology against destitute people – many of whom are fleeing the effects of similar drone technology deployed in their home countries – demonstrates that the border is simply an extension of global militarised policing apparatus. It is designed to exclude the world's racialised poor from the resources Europe looted from them.

Everywhere border

European border controls are not limited to Europe though. States increasingly 'export' their borders so that migrants are stopped before they even make it here. For instance, under the guise of aid, the UK provide technology, funding and training to Moroccan and Tunisian border forces to stop and return central and West African migrants before they attempt to cross to Europe.[6] The EU has facilitated the G5 Sahel Cross-Border Force between Burkina Faso, Chad, Mali, Mauritania and Niger which is a combination of militarised counterterrorism and anti-migration forces whose job is to prevent the movement of mainly Black African Muslims into North Africa.[7]

Those who make it past those armed forces, through thousands of miles of often trackless desert, to coastal countries like Libya, then risk enslavement, trafficking, sexual violence

---

5 https://businessinsider.com/uk-deploys-military-drone-migrants-english-channel-record-crossings-2020-9?r=US&IR=T (accessed March 2021).

6 https://privacyinternational.org/long-read/2780/project-hunter-uk-programme-exporting-its-border-abroad (accessed January 2021).

7 Harsha Walia, *Border and Rule: Global Migration, Capitalism, and the Rise of Racist Nationalism* (UK: Haymarket Books, 2021), p. 221.

and in many cases, death.[8] If they survive and make it to the sea, the journey to Europe across the Mediterranean swallows thousands more without trace every year. These conditions are a stark reminder that refugee experiences are not equal. Anti-Black racism enables Arabs in states like Libya to dehumanise and exploit the labour of Black Africans, even as they also experience Europe's border violence and Islamophobia themselves. Collaboration in racial violence by so-called Muslim countries therefore multiplies the factors of persecution Black Muslims face even before they get to Europe.

From the hostile environment and deportations, to drone technology and training foreign border forces, Europe pours billions of pounds into keeping migrants out. But none of these measures 'work' because they do not end the causes of displacement, they just criminalise the displaced. For example, drought, floods and deforestation displace one person every one to two seconds.[9] These climate catastrophes are caused by historic European extraction of crops, as well as current corporate land-grabs and structural-adjustment-policies which border controls do nothing to address. Likewise, immigration controls do not resolve the imperialist wars and subsequent conflicts which displace people every day.

Locked in and locked out

In 2019, US President Donald Trump proposed to designate all undocumented migrants to the US as 'enemy combatants' and send them to Guantanamo Bay.[10] Treating refugees as a ter-

---

8 https://time.com/longform/african-slave-trade/ (accessed March 2021).

9 Walia, *Border and Rule*, p. 70–73.

10 https://theguardian.com/us-news/2019/nov/13/trump-proposed-sending-undocumented-migrants-to-guantanamo-anonymous-book-claims (accessed March 2021).

rorising military force may seem astounding but it is already well-established in Britain where detention centres modelled on military internment camps house asylum-seeking people indefinitely.[11] Tens of thousands of people seeking asylum, renewing visas or who have the wrong documentation are imprisoned in what Britain calls Immigration Removal Centres (IRCs). Scholar, Liz Fekete argues that IRCs have established 'a separate prison regime for asylum seekers' which developed from military concentration camps built to detain Afrikaners during Britain's Boer War in what is now South Africa.[12] The UK is the only European nation that has no maximum limit on such detention. This is agonising for those detained who never know when they might be released, or what will happen next, leading to high levels of self-harm, suicide, depression and anxiety in IRCs.

Moreover, it is common knowledge that women and children held at Yarl's Wood detention centre have faced sexual and other forms of abuse, and that detention of pregnant women has contravened Home Office guidelines. Multiple people have also died after concerns were ignored by healthcare staff.[13] This system has no regard for human rights. It terrorises and neglects people to make them compliant with their deportation. Physical abuse is also common, in the words of a former detainee, 'whilst I was in detention I was provided with a bed – it was a metal bed without a mattress. When I tried to complain about it, I received terrible beatings [by guards]. I was kept in isolation for over a week . . . I can't even go into some details which will just make me cry.'[14]

---

11 Liz Fekete, *A Suitable Enemy: Racism, Migration and Islamophobia in Europe* (London: Pluto, 2009), p. 148.

12 Ibid.

13 Leah Cowan, *Border Nation: A Story of Migration* (London: Pluto, 2021), p. 108.

14 https://detainedvoices.com/page/5/ (accessed March 2021).

Detained people resist these conditions through protest and food strikes almost constantly, and others participate in solidarity protests from outside. However, the detention-centre-complex does not stand alone, it is part of the prison system, and shares similarities with the counterterror system specifically in its defiance of legal norms. Therefore, opposition to immigration detention centres must extend to all forms of caging and policing people, especially as they are often run by the same corporations.

G4S – mentioned previously as a provider of private military services in Afghanistan – is one of the multinational corporations who, along with Serco and Sodexo, manage 14 UK prisons – 18% of the prison population. With Mitie and GEO Group, they also run every detention centre in the UK except Morton Hall. They profit through multi-million-pound government contracts, and by cutting spending on hygienic conditions or medical care for detainees, and paying them £1 an hour to clean and cook, or 80p a day for a working week in prison.[15] Over 300 businesses use such labour in the UK.[16]

Although breakdown of IRC detainees by religion are hard to find, we know that over 50% of those at Brook House and Tinsley House detention centres are Muslim.[17] Like the 15% of UK prison population who are Muslim, they also face unique harms. The government's own documents show that the scale of Muslims in detention means there is insufficient space to accommodate Jummah prayers in multiple IRCs.[18] Unhygienic conditions have also forced Muslims to pray next to open toilets

---

15 Cowan, *Border Nation*, p. 12; and James Trafford, *The Empire at Home: Internal Colonies and the End of Britain* (London: Pluto, 2020), p. 78.

16 Trafford, *End of Empire*, p. 78.

17 https://law.ox.ac.uk/research-subject-groups/centre-criminology/centreborder-criminologies/blog/2020/01/religion (accessed March 2021).

18 Stephen Shaw, Review into the Welfare in Detention of Vulnerable Persons (London: Home Office, 2016), p. 138.

– judged a human rights abuse by a High Court in 2018.[19] Islamophobia is not only used to justify border policing then, border controls harm Muslims in specific and disproportionate ways due to the numbers detained. This is a reminder that any movement to aid refugees and migrants must work actively against Islamophobia in all its guises.

The stated aim of IRCs is to hold people for eventual deportation. The government charter deportation flights with private companies who have been known to make up to £12,000 per person deported.[20] Such forced removals, as the government calls them, essentially kidnap people from IRCs, immigration raids and, increasingly, people convicted of unrelated crimes, even those made homeless, and notoriously the Windrush generation, onto secretive flights in violent conditions usually hidden from everyday flight passengers.[21] Some do not even have time to contact lawyers or friends. They are often gagged, bound, sometimes even drugged, facing armed guards, dogs and more to get them on these flights.[22] In 2010, Jimmy Mubenga was murdered when three G4S guards used extreme force to restrain him on a British Airways flight to Angola. No one at G4S or in government was ever held responsible for his death. To what ends is such violence necessary?

Preserving pillaged resources

In her book, *(B)ordering Britain*, Nadine El-Enany traces how British immigration laws have always intended a hostile envi-

---

19   https://gardencourtchambers.co.uk/news/high-court-rules-on-discriminatory-and-unlawful-practices-at-brook-house-muslim-immigration-detainees-forced-to-worship-in-degrading-conditions (accessed March 2021).

20   https://theguardian.com/politics/2020/feb/12/deportation-flights-for-37-people-cost-home-office-443000 (accessed March 2021).

21   Trafford, *End of Empire*, p. 136.

22   Fekete, *Suitable Enemy*, p. 138.

ronment for racialised people.[23] The 1948 British Nationality Act (BNA), which granted British citizenship to all Commonwealth citizens, enabled people from the Caribbean and South Asia to move to Britain and work – famously the reason the Windrush generation and those like my grandparents arrived in the UK. But the BNA was never meant to enable our movement. Instead, as Nadine told me, it was passed to signal that empire was still strong despite recent losses, and to enable outward movement of white Britons to settle in colonies: 'there wasn't even a sense anybody would arrive . . . so when the Windrush arrived officials were shocked, and they did what they could to stop people coming'. This included techniques still used today such as forcing 'source' countries to make it harder for people to leave, neglecting migrants by refusing housing and employment rights, and even drafting plans to move them elsewhere.

So, far from signalling to new post-Brexit trends, the operation of the hostile environment is a continuation of older controls. In Nadine's words, immigration controls have always attempted to create 'as white supremacist a Britain as possible, short of introducing an explicit "White Britain policy"'.[24] In fact, every piece of immigration legislation passed since 1948 tried to restrict access to citizenship to white people. This culminated in the 1981 Act which limited it to people whose parents were born in Britain, who were much more likely to be white than racialised migrants at that time. Such legislation signified that the resources inside Britain – plundered from across the world – are the right of white Britons only, making immigration policy an extended defence of colonial spoils.

Britain's enrichment through colonisation is not only 'in the past', either. Nadine reminds me it is reaped and felt every day.

---

23   Nadine El-Enany, *(B)ordering Britain: Law, race and empire* (Manchester: Manchester University Press, 2020).

24   Ibid., p. 53.

For instance, the money from the government's billion-pound bail-out to 'compensate' slave owners after the abolition of slavery has been invested in institutions, commerce, welfare and corporations around us today from banks to Universities. Meanwhile Caribbean rainforests and soil remain devastated by the plantations enslaved people were forced to work on which restructured land and water use for production of tea, sugar, tobacco and cotton for British and international markets. This has left much of the Caribbean vulnerable to the impact of hurricanes and flooding today which displace millions of people. Such catastrophes are caused by rising sea temperatures and levels that are a result of global warming caused by the Global North.[25] So, wealth from colonial plunder, slavery and imperialism is not only baked into the bricks and mortar of Britain, its extraction also underpins the levels of global displacement today.

Border controls aim to 'secure' the resources gained through colonialism from the ex-colonised who are left to its lethal consequences. Therefore, when politicians and journalists talk of barbaric terrorists teeming at the edges of Western states, the terrorisation of colonial white supremacy that shapes Britain today is hidden and, in Ambalavaner Sivanandan's words, a racism is produced 'that cannot tell a settler from an immigrant, an immigrant from an asylum seeker, an asylum seeker from a Muslim, a Muslim from a terrorist. All of us non-whites, at first sight, are terrorists or illegals. We wear our passports on our faces – or, lacking them, we are faceless, destitute…'[26]

---

25   https://disasterdisplacement.org/portfolio-item/fma-caribbean (accessed March 2021).

26   https://irr.org.uk/article/racism-liberty-and-the-war-on-terror/ (accessed March 2021).

Sexual metaphors

Not only are migrants and refugees imagined as threats to jobs and security, but also to white women and girls. For instance, when unconfirmed stories of 'mobs' of Muslim asylum-seekers participating in sexual assaults in Germany circulated widely in 2016,[27] calls for their deportation were immediate. In Sweden, the reports led to introduction of classes especially for refugee boys and men on sex and gender equality.[28] Both cases reflect the way that sexual violence is often constructed as a uniquely Muslim/migrant import, despite being a normalised part of European life. In the UK this is manifest most clearly in the narrative about Asian 'grooming gangs' which creates the idea of sexually predatory Muslim men whose deviance is 'foreign'.

In fact, men with dual nationalities in the Rochdale and Rotherham grooming gang cases had their British citizenships stripped. Such a penalty has never been issued to white perpetrators of child sexual exploitation, despite the majority of such cases being perpetrated by white men. The border is therefore used both to punish racialised sexual offenders in unique ways; and to imagine sexual violence as external to Europe, justifying more border controls. It especially justifies policing of male migrants who are often discussed as 'feigning' vulnerability or pretending to be children. In 2021, Priti Patel stated that 87% of people who entered the UK by boat the previous year were men, and '74% were aged between 18–39'. She asked, 'where are the vulnerable women and children?'[29] insinuating

27 https://welt.de/vermischtes/article150593304/Ploetzlich-spuerte-ich-eine-Hand-an-meinem-Po.html (accessed March 2021).
28 https://thelocal.se/20160118/swedish-campaigners-teach-refugee-boys-about-sex/ (accessed March 2021).
29 https://gov.uk/government/speeches/home-secretarys-statement-on-the-new-plan-for-immigration (accessed March 2021).

that asylum-seeking men are *not* vulnerable and in fact actively threatening, especially by referring to their 'virile' age-bracket.

While sexual violence is systematic in Britain, it is only taken seriously on a selective basis. Labour Party politicians write headlines declaring 'Pakistani men are raping white girls', and Tory MPs claim the UK has a specific problem with 'sick Asian paedophiles'. But the majority of women in UK prisons have experienced domestic and sexual abuse. Women detained in Yarl's Wood are sexually abused by guards. Sexual assault is normalised in private and state schools.[30] And, as the police murder of Sarah Everard and violence at subsequent vigils showed in 2021, the police are institutionally sexually violent.[31] In terms of grooming gangs specifically, the Home Office itself found 'group-based offenders are most commonly white'.[32] Yet child sex abuse rings in Cornwall and Devon, who used the same methods as those in Rochdale and Rotherham, never received national coverage.

I am not interested in arguing that 'white men sexually abuse women, too', or in suggesting the normalised nature of sexual abuse minimises its violence. Instead, I am concerned that the narrative of Muslim men as exceptionally sexually violent has been cynically used to justify border policing on grounds of protecting white women and girls from a presumed sexual threat. The focus on 'white women' and 'Asian paedophiles', taps into historic tropes of non-white male migrants muddying the waters of whiteness through rape – a trope that has seen many Black men lynched throughout US history, and over-policed in the UK.

---

30   https://theguardian.com/society/2021/mar/27/sexual-abuse-rife-in-state-schools-say-police (accessed March 2021).

31   https://sistersuncut.org/2021/03/15/our-response-to-boris-statement-no-more-police/ (accessed March 2021).

32   https://theguardian.com/commentisfree/2020/dec/19/home-office-report-grooming-gangs-not-muslim (accessed March 2021).

Just as Muslim women's bodies are discussed to reflect anxieties about the future of the nation being tainted; protecting white women's bodies is imagined as protecting the reproduction of white Britishness from 'foreigners'. But this is not a concern for survivors. In fact, survivors of sexual violence are generally overlooked in the obsession with grooming gangs. In Rotherham there have been constant far-right rallies, attacks on mosques, Muslim businesses and taxi drivers; Muslim girls have been threatened with 'revenge' rape, and 81-year-old Muhsin Ahmed was murdered in 2015 by two white men who called him a 'groomer'.[33] None of this brings justice or healing to survivors of sexual abuse, just as deportation of abusers does not address the conditions that made girls vulnerable in the first place.

Concern for survivors would instead lead to eradication of the conditions of poverty and systemic misogyny that make women and girls vulnerable. It would lead to the dismantlement of a justice system more concerned with property crimes than abuse of children. It would require funding child protection and sexual violence services gutted by austerity. And an end to criminalising working-class children – when one victim of abuse was found in a derelict house with a group of men in South Yorkshire, police deemed her 'drunk and disorderly' and took no action until after years of abuse when she was recognised as 'vulnerable'.[34] Genuine concern would also recognise that non-white children are victims of sexual violence too, but the public consciousness cannot comprehend that, say, a Muslim boy, could be a victim of sexual abuse deserving of support.

Focus on Muslim 'grooming gangs' simply externalises and essentialises sexual violence into racialised Others. Deportation

---

33   Ibid.

34   https://irr.org.uk/article/asian-grooming-gangs-media-state-and-the-far-right/ (accessed March 2021).

of perpetrators also demonstrates that the hostile environment is understood not only to secure us against Muslims at our borders, but that Muslims already 'inside' them can be kicked out if the state sees fit. Citizenship is a gift bestowed out of generosity and removed upon bad behaviour, upholding the border as a tool of racialised coercion for both those inside and outside of it.

Are we safer now?

The construction of Muslims as terrorist, misogynistic outsiders has proved extremely profitable for corporations that thrive on militarising borders, and for states that use it to mask their structural and historic violence. Therefore, like all parts of the security apparatus, despite the rhetoric, borders have not made most of us safer; for many, they have necessitated death.

We must wrest back the language of safety on our own terms. It is not enough to reform immigration legislation or end the 'hostile environment'; we must end the imperialism, policing, arms trade, global warming and drone-war that displace people in the first place. And we must refuse the notion of borders altogether because when we connect 'here' to 'there', 'us' to 'them', and 'now' to 'then', it becomes clear that borders are neither necessary nor useful to most of us. They simply allow colonial states to hoard resources from those most ravaged by the consequences of their extraction; and to create revenue-streams for multinational corporations.

Islamophobia is upheld by and upholds that process, so dismantling it requires demolition of borders and categories of migrant, refugee, citizen and asylum-seeker. Our fight for safety must be unconditional safety for all, beginning from the most oppressed and maligned of the dispossessed.

Shukri Abdi, a twelve-year-old Somali refugee, may not have been killed crossing the border, but the spectre of death haunted her from displacement via post-colonial war, to refugee camp, to white supremacist British institutions, and investigation by police notorious for neglecting Black communities. When we demand justice for her death, we are asking for another world. So, the question is not, 'how do we build a world without borders?' But, 'what would it take for Shukri Abdi to not only have lived, but thrived?'

Chapter 9

The feminist and queer-friendly West? The patriarchal rest?

> Could we not leave veils and vocations of saving others behind
> and instead train our sights on ways to make the world a more
> just place? – Lila Abu-Lughod[1]

Images of Muslim women in hijab and niqab permeate our
day: splayed under newspaper headlines, moving through the
landscapes of TV documentaries, and accompanying stories as
varied as COVID, women's rights, terrorism, the EU or unemployment rates. So far in this book we have also established how
Muslim women are viewed as crucial links in counterterrorism,
integration and counter-extremism initiatives which see our
homes, languages, dress and birth-rates requiring regulation or
co-option.

Islamophobia has always had specific implications and
manifestations for women. However, it is generally only
acknowledged as harming Muslim women when it takes the
form of explicit attacks. And in such instances, the solution to

---

1 Lila Abu-Lughod, 'Do Muslim women really need saving? Anthropological reflections on cultural relativism and its Others', *American Anthropologist*, Vol. 104:3,
2002, 783–90, p. 789.

aggression is usually proposed through urging Muslim women to break stereotypes and challenge narratives, or celebrate our inclusion in marketing campaigns – from Nike hijabs to H&M adverts, and music videos.

Such conversations and projects avoid seriously considering what conditions are required for Muslim women to be safe in our everyday lives. Moreover, they misdirect our attention from the fact that it is state-sanctioned surveillance and mutation of well-being services into policing operations that makes our safety impossible. Our hijabs are pulled off in the street because they are criminalised at state-level; and we are called terrorists on the bus, because we are constructed as terrorists in public policy.

But Muslim women's experiences of violence are instead deliberately misread as somehow our own fault, stemming from a cultural submissiveness and shyness – hence the incessant focus on breaking stereotypes rather than systems. Alternatively, any violence facing Muslim women is presumed an outcome of patriarchal Muslim men and Islam, not any other contexts or material conditions. This means that even our oppression is often weaponised against us to justify criminalisation of our families and communities in the name of liberating us. There-fore, in all the rhetorical concern for Muslim women, we find an utter lack of care.

Exceptionally patriarchal?

Hijabs, niqabs, female-genital-mutilation, forced marriages, honour killings, strict dads and overbearing brothers are the tropes used to refer to an apparently culturally-specific, barbaric misogyny that comes with Muslim presence in the West. These issues are raised in everyday conversations as fact. Often, the people who bring them up do not extend their concern for Muslim women to our experiences of wars, the criminal justice system, national security policing or our disproportionate experiences of poverty, austerity and immigration detention. Instead, the violence Muslim women face is only viewed as important when attributable to Muslim men and Islam.

Professor Fatima El-Tayeb argues that this is because Muslim presence in Europe is 'framed not in the language of race, religion or nation, but in that of culture and gender'[2] – the essential distinction between Muslims and Europe is presented as one where violence and patriarchy belong to Muslim culture/Islam and are external to 'the West'. Western states thereby define themselves as not only peaceful, but inherently feminist, and equal, since misogyny is framed as a cultural defect, not an operation of power. Consequently, conversations about Muslim women's victimhood and Muslim men's misogyny are less to do with Muslims, than they are to do with constructing 'the West'. And they do not improve Muslim women's lives, but instead cloud understandings of violence in general.

For instance, 'honour crimes' are framed as a gendered form of violence specific to Muslim men that occur when Muslim women and girls behave in ways they disapprove of. But if domestic violence in general is a result of men's attempts to exert control over women's behaviour, how useful is it to distinguish 'honour crimes' from other violent manifestations of masculinity? Men who domestically abuse current or former partners kill two women a week in the UK, while twelve women a year are killed in 'honour killings'.[3] Neither number is justifiable, but the smaller figure is sensationalised and the bigger

---

2   Fatima El-Tayeb, *European Others: Queering Ethnicity in Postnational Europe* (Minnesota: University of Minnesota Press, 2011), p. 83.

3   https://lwa.org.uk/understanding-abuse/statistics/ (accessed March 2021).

not deemed an emergency. Moreover the term 'honour killing' attributes violence to a cultural mentality of 'honour', which obscures the fact that patriarchal violence and femicide are systemic and political.

For example, many women are forced to rely on abusive partners due to poverty and state neglect. The majority of women in UK prisons are survivors of domestic violence which reveals that they are more often punished, than protected, when they seek state intervention.[4] Indeed a justice-system that over-criminalises Black and brown women and victim-blames all women, leaves us unable to seek its protection from abusive situations that may lead to our deaths. Additionally, undocumented and migrant women who call outside institutions to intervene in abusive situations could end up being deported or detained themselves.[5]

In the case of Muslim women specifically, as much as the state professes that Muslim men's violence is a major concern to it, structural Islamophobia often forces Muslim women who do experience domestic violence at the hands of Muslim men to stay in those situations. This is because the racialisation of Muslims as threats means that if she involves police, social workers or other formal institutions into her family life, it could lead to her or her partner being reported to Prevent, incarcerated, or even her children being removed, or her citizenship stripped. Racialising Muslims as exceptionally patriarchal is not only racist then, it also obscures the crucial connection between interpersonal and state violence that means the state is directly involved in women's murders through the criminal justice system which is an accomplice of sexual violence, not 'protector' from it.

---

4   http://prisonreformtrust.org.uk/PressPolicy/News/vw/1/ItemID/494   (accessed July 2021).

5   Ibid.

Moral panics about Muslim men's misogyny also do not protect Muslim women from it where it does exist. For instance, if a Muslim woman speaks about Muslim men as patriarchal or wants to discuss cases of sexual or misogynistic abuse, our statements are weaponised against us to prove how much Muslims deserve criminalisation and how in need of civilising we are. Far from liberating Muslim women from any patriarchy, this means Islamophobia colludes with patriarchy to force Muslim women to maintain a silence about gendered injustice so it cannot be weaponised to worsen our communal lives.

To take a personal example, my mother once got into a disagreement with our local mosque committee because of an inadequate quality of prayer space for women. When I tweeted about their exchange a BBC reporter instantly contacted me. I had never had such a swift response from the BBC for any tweets about racism or Islamophobia, so I knew immediately that the reporter did not have either my mother's or my needs in mind. Their coverage would not grant us better quality of prayer space or facilitate our ease of worship because such priorities would not be considered valid demands for Muslim women to make in the first place. Instead, the story would probably evidence how misogynistic and backwards Muslims are – proof that harsher counter-extremism policing is needed to tackle the 'hateful' beliefs of our mosque board. If the mosque wasn't already Prevent funded, it would be, and our Friday khutbah (sermon) would become replete with depoliticising rhetoric.

Far from assisting Muslim women, Islamophobic obsession with 'patriarchal Muslim men' therefore colludes with patriarchal dynamics to punish, exclude and silence Muslim women, especially when we do experience misogyny and gendered injustice.

Feminism's collusion with Islamophobia

Due to imagining Muslim men and Islam as inherently patriarchal, Muslim women's liberation is also imagined as directly connected to us assimilating into European secular whiteness, rather than to attaining justice on our own terms. For example, mainstream feminist narratives about our liberation rarely include toppling white supremacy. Instead, the 'success stories' of Ex-Muslim women like Ayaan Hirsi Ali demonstrate the pinnacle of the white feminist fantasy for us: leaving Islam marks our fullest freedom – often represented by removal of hijab. Indeed, it is revealing that Muslim women's dress is simultaneously constructed as the most significant symbol of how 'free' *and* how 'civilised' we are. Our own relationships to what we wear are made irrelevant. Furthermore, the similarity between 'the Islamophobe' who pulls off a women's hijab, and the feminist and/or assimilationist discourses that seek to, are often glossed over.

Much is made of UK Prime Minister, Boris Johnson, comparing women wearing niqabs to 'letterboxes' and 'bank robbers'. His objectifying and criminalising remarks sparked a 375% rise in recorded Islamophobic attacks on women.[6] Despite this state-sanctioned violence being condemned by many people, it is usually accepted when facilitated through the law. For instance, Prevent and counter-extremism make all public services target, criminalise and exclude Muslim women for what we wear. Yet this systemic violence rouses little public outrage about misogyny or Islamophobia, despite being within the same continuum as more visible street violence and verbal slurs. In part, public indifference to this is shaped by a longer

---

6   Mustafa, *Gendered Islamophobia in Europe*, p. 6.

history where removal of Muslim women's dress has been constructed as liberatory.

During the late 1950s in the Algerian war for independence, French colonisers organised 'unveiling ceremonies' where Algerian men were rounded up and brought to witness the 'unveiling' of Algerian women by the wives of French military officers. These ceremonies were intended as symbolic demonstrations of the success of French forces.[7] They also satiated a patriarchal fantasy of 'accessing' Muslim women's bodies, and in doing so, 'emasculating' Muslim men. The women's voices, needs and wants, were irrelevant; some were even paid to participate.[8]

Since Europeans began travelling to and colonising the so-called Middle East, Ottoman Empire, North Africa and South Asia, depictions of 'the East' were explicitly gendered and sexualised. European men were often unable to access the spaces women socialised, so they fantasised 'the harem', and 'hammams' as places of transgressive sexual abandon. Photographers paid women to model in costumes with props based on their own imaginings of the East, which they then circulated throughout Europe.[9] Even European women who met and evangelised Muslim women in their own homes reinforced the dominant image of exotic mystery.[10] Therefore, nineteenth-century European accounts depict Muslim women as simultaneously 'objects of pity, deprived of liberty', but also possessing a 'libidinous nature'.

---

7   Abu-Lughod, *Do Muslim women need saving?*
8   https://newyorker.com/books/second-read/colonial-postcards-and-women-as-props-for-war-making (accessed February 2021).
9   Ibid.
10   Thisaranie Herath, 'Women and Orientalism: 19th Century representations of the harem by European female travellers and Ottoman women', *Constellations*, Vol. 7:10, 2016, p. 32.

In 2001, Oprah Winfrey 'unveiled' an Afghan woman on a stage in New York City as part of an event to end violence against women and girls. This unveiling symbolised another imperialist conquest that we were told would liberate Muslim women – images of women in burqas were widely circulated that year to whet the public appetite for the invasion of Afghanistan which was also constructed as a force for women's liberation.[11] The subsequent decades of war, displacement and destruction are rarely discussed as processes that oppress and violate Muslim women.

In fact, mainstream feminism often pitches equality on neoliberal, imperialist and ethnonationalist terms. It celebrates women fighting for state militaries, taking up positions in imperialist state governance or becoming CEOs for corporations that exploit the labour of women in the Global South. 'Equality' on these terms leaves most women on earth exploited, deprived, displaced, occupied, undocumented and persecuted. It simply replaces one coloniser with another – colluding with racial violence as French military wives did in the 1950s.

Additionally, in all this focus on dress, Muslim women who do not wear hijab or other visible markers of their Muslimness are made invisible. At the same time, the static way hijab is depicted excludes styles more common in different African traditions. This means both Muslims and non-Muslims erase many Black Muslim women as Muslim through racially categorising their head coverings as broadly 'African' – an erasure that relies on the wildly ahistorical construction of 'African' as non-Muslim. Black Muslim women subsequently experience the above-mentioned tropes entangled with historic constructions of Black women as aggressive, masculine and asexual, as well as licentious and

---

11   Abu-Lughod, *Do Muslim women really need saving?*

innately promiscuous. Removal of their hijab or niqab therefore reproduces a historic pattern of Black women's bodies being deliberately violated for white consumption, voyeurism and profit.

When women's liberation is disconnected from our material conditions, our lives are not made more liveable, instead we are reduced to symbolic meaning. This underpins the introduction of laws banning hijabs and niqabs from being worn in Belgium, Bulgaria, Denmark, France, Luxemburg, Austria, Norway, Netherlands and Switzerland.[12] Sometimes these bans are hidden within a 'general ban' – for example in 2021 the European Union's highest court ruled that private employers throughout the EU can ban 'religious dress',[13] but in practice such bans disproportionately target Muslim women in the name of secularism, maintaining 'neutrality', security or protecting Muslim women. Switzerland's ban on niqabs in public spaces was passed on International Women's Day in 2021 and backed by 51% of Swiss voters, but only around 30 women in the country wear niqab.[14] Meanwhile, wearing facial masks due to COVID-19 at the time was mandatory. This reinforces how little these bans have to do with freedom, security or feminism. Instead, they aim to increase support for governments through brazen ethnonationalism and Islamophobia.

Yet the lives of the women affected are fundamentally altered by the state removing their right to choose their own clothes. Such bans ironically push Muslim women out of public participation and employment. And even while a niqab ban does not

---

12   Mustafa, *Gendered Islamophobia in Europe*, p. 8.

13   https://hrw.org/news/2021/07/19/european-union-court-oks-bans-religious-dress-work (accessed July 2021).

14   https://metro.co.uk/2021/03/08/switzerland-to-ban-the-burqa-and-niqab-in-public-places-14205555/ (accessed March 2021).

target all visibly Muslim women, we all become hyper-visible as problems. Even public debates *about* bans impact our visibility and thus our access to support, space and safety. In 2017, the UK school's inspectorate, Ofsted, announced they would begin asking primary school children why they wore headscarves to determine if they were being 'sexualised'. Consequently, Muslim girls who were already seen as suspicious through Prevent, became even less able to experience school as a place of learning, and more as a place of policing. Such exceptional targeting of headscarves was not because of a concern about sexualisation – arguably every gendered form of clothing can be considered sexualising (skirts? dresses? bikinis?). This was just another effort to problematise and police Muslims.

A deep anxiety about the West itself underpins these interventions into Muslim women's dress. The fact we might want to cover our bodies is unthinkable because it disrupts the idea that secular, liberal notions of 'freedom' are universal. In not equating our freedom to making ourselves intelligible to a sexualising white male gaze, we are 'unbearable'.[15] If so-called liberation movements cannot confront this, they do not seek our liberation *from* injustice, but our liberation *into* coloniality.

Sexual deviants

Alongside patriarchy, homophobia is deemed a uniquely Muslim trait, and further proof of Muslim backwardness. Consider British media coverage of the prolonged and visible 'row' focused on schools in Birmingham in 2019. The circumstances invoked the Trojan Horse affair of 2015 and its image of 'hardline Muslim men'. But this time, those men were presented as

15   Sahar Ghumkhor, *The Political Psychology of the Veil: The Impossible Body* (UK: Palgrave Macmillan, 2020).

parents protesting the 'No Outsiders' programme. No Outsiders was an educational resource developed by schoolteacher, Andrew Moffat, as a series of storybooks to teach pupils about the 'protected characteristics' of the 2010 Equality Act. One of these included sexual orientation. Media coverage, therefore, centred on the fact that most pupils and parents at the schools protesting No Outsiders being taught, were Muslim. This presented the row as an issue of furious Muslim patriarchs protesting 'inclusive' ideals of toleration and queer rights. In the words of the former head of Ofsted, they needed to realise 'they're living in this country – we are a liberal country'.[16]

We do not need to deny the presence of homophobia in the protests to recognise that this presentation of the row tapped into what queer theorist, Jasbir Puar, calls 'homonationalism'. This is the process by which LGBTQ+ rights are used for nationalist and racist ends. For instance, to depict violent border controls as queer-friendly policies against 'homophobic migrants and Muslims'. In the case of the No Outsiders row, many LGBTQ+ individuals and organisations signed a 'not-in-my-name' open-letter addressing this.

'The spotlight on Muslim communities and the moral panic that has ensued demonstrates that Muslims are an easy target for accusations of homophobia, which can be used to demonise entire communities . . . we condemn the cynical use of our identities as a form of dog-whistle racism, which is being mobilised to justify harmful policies of state surveillance and the criminalisation of Muslim communities'.[17]

---

16 https://blogs.soas.ac.uk/gender-studies/2019/05/30/its-ok-to-be-different-prevent-british-values-and-the-birmingham-lgbt-lessons-row/ (accessed March 2021).

17 https://independent.co.uk/voices/letters/lgbt-no-outsiders-rse-birmingham-muslim-prevent-values-a9092781.html (accessed January 2021).

Educator and writer, Latifa Akay, explains to me that 'there is heavy conservatism and homophobia in British society' and the externalisation of homophobia onto Muslims is yet another attempt to define Britain as 'more advanced' than 'the Other' who requires civilising. She added, 'some of the schools involved in this case had alienated their Muslim communities by approaching teaching LGBTQ-inclusive curricula as part of their counter-extremism work meeting obligations under the Prevent Duty. At Parkfield school this was described by senior leadership as part of the strategy to 'reduce radicalisation'. The irony is extraordinary. Teaching children that 'it's okay to be different' while criminalising those racialised as 'different' reflects the superficiality of the project.

The state promotes a form of LGBTQ+ rights that are absorbed into white nationalist 'British values' and a policing apparatus. They are therefore, in Latifa's words, 'reserved for those LGBT+ people who fit within the state's ever-shrinking and racist construction of citizenship . . . not to those who experience the violence of the British state.' For instance, people seeking asylum on the basis of sexual orientation are frequently deported and detained by the British state. So, like the rhetorical concern for Muslim women, the state's 'concern' about homophobia masks its ethnonationalist violence. Moreover, the reason many people seek asylum on grounds of sexual orientation is because of legislation prohibiting homosexuality which, in most places globally, comes from British colonialism. And yet its existence is now used to exemplify non-Western 'backwardness'.

Such colonial legislation was passed because just as Europeans viewed Muslim women as sexually licentious, Muslim men were viewed as having untameable, deviant sexual appetites that needed regulating. In fact, as part of the orientalist myth, the 'Muslim world' was viewed as a site of homosexual activity.

Georg Klauda writes that, 'countless writers and artists such as Andre Gide, Oscar Wilde, Edward M Forster and Jean Genet made pilgrimages in the 19th and 20th centuries from homophobic Europe to Algeria, Morocco, Egypt and various other Arab countries' where they felt they would not face the same ghettoisation and discrimination as in Europe for their homosexuality. In fact, they saw those places as homosexually permissive.[18]

Clearly, European narratives about what makes Muslims outsiders have been constantly in flux. When racialising us as sexually deviant marked us as backwards, we were imagined as virulently homosexual; and now that homophobia is the mark of backwardness, we are ascribed with that. In either case, the treatment of Muslim and LGBTQ people shows we are actually irrelevant to Western states in their pursuit to define themselves in ways that obscure their violence.

Care at your convenience

Whether 'rapists', 'honour killers', 'homophobes' or, 'sexually repressed', the construction of Muslim masculinity as barbaric, and Muslim women as inherently oppressed has little to do with Muslims, or a concern for gender or sexual justice. Instead, these discourses externalise gendered and sexual violence to hide the realities of Britain and other Western state's latent misogyny, rape culture and structural violence against women and queer people at the hands of austerity, deportation, detention, policing, imperialism and militarism. By placing the origin of gendered and sexual violence within Muslim religion/culture, like 'terrorism', its root causes are depoliticised and only Muslims are held accountable for it.

18   https://mronline.org/2010/12/08/globalizing-homophobia/ (accessed November 2020).

We are deployed, misused, blamed, objectified, covered, uncovered, spoken over and spoken for, but never allowed to exist on our own terms and speak about the ways we are harmed without fear of further harm. To create a world free of gendered and sexual violence we need to recognise the state, capitalism and coloniality as primary perpetrators. When we centre the needs and safety of the most marginalised, invisible and 'impossible' Muslim women and girls, we begin to see this very clearly.

Chapter 10

Islamophobia's beneficiaries

As I began my research for this chapter in November 2020, I was interrupted by the forces I had intended to scrutinise. I received an email from Fiona Hamilton, the 'Crime and Security' editor of the *Times*, a right-wing British newspaper owned by billionaire, Rupert Murdoch. Hamilton asked me to comment for a piece she wanted to write about concerns raised by the neoconservative think tank, the Henry Jackson Society (HJS), who 'questioned' my appropriateness to present a BBC Radio 4 documentary on poetry that week. Who are the Henry Jackson Society? Why did they care about my radio show? And why was an editor of 'crime and security' worried enough to write about it?

Hamilton told me the HJS had no issue with my programme, they just felt my 'affiliation' with the advocacy group CAGE meant it was inappropriate for me to be on the BBC (despite CAGE having been on the BBC numerous times themselves). As discussed in Chapter 6, CAGE are a Muslim-led grassroots human rights organisation working against the injustices of the War on Terror and therefore often face charges such as Hamilton's description of them as 'an organisation accused in the past of being apologists for terrorists'. I can only presume that made me terrorist-apologist-aligned and therefore a danger to Radio 4 listeners.

I never replied to Hamilton and no article ever went up. But finding myself on the receiving end of a coordinated Islamophobic smear by a well-established think tank and a right-wing news corporation left me hypervigilant. My body went into fight-or-flight mode when I received the email and adrenaline surged into my bloodstream. With my arms physically shaking, I spent hours typing a draft response to an article that never appeared and spent a week or more in anticipation of it being published. In those moments, the agendas of private profit-making corporations and global industries that thrive on Islamophobia played out in my nervous system and my heartbeat.

Think tanks

The Henry Jackson Society was formed in 2005 at my alma mater, home of the best-dressed liberal racism, Cambridge University. The HJS offices are now at Millbank, neighbouring central government offices. HJS have chaired All-Party Parliamentary Groups (APPGs) on policymaking and received millions in funding from across the US and UK. Their members include government ministers like Michael Gove, and former heads of the CIA. As such an institutionalised organisation so close to the establishment, why do they care what someone like me says, or who I affiliate with?

The first clue is that their members include the likes of Douglas Murray, who has called for 'conditions to be made harder for Muslims across the board'. It also includes William Shawcross – currently the chosen reviewer of Prevent – who called Guantanamo Bay a 'model' of justice and defended the use of water-boarding.[1] It is no surprise HJS's own co-founder

1   https://standpointmag.co.uk/counterpoints-may-11-model-justice-william-shawcross-guantanamo-bay-military-courts/ (accessed March 2021); https://amp.thenationalnews.com/arts-culture/books/justice-and-the-enemy-due-process-must-yield-to-terror-fight-1.407912 (accessed March 2021).

has called the HJS 'far-right, anti-Muslim racist' since leaving.[2] Further, the HJS Statement of Principles is signed by multiple journalists associated with the *Times*, and by Irwin Stelzer, a close advisor to Rupert Murdoch who owns the newspaper.[3] This partially explains why Hamilton took the concerns of such an Islamophobic group to be a legitimate basis for an article. These connections between news media corporations, think tanks, government ministers, journalists and international elites, demonstrate that there is a network of stakeholders invested in the creation of Islamophobic narratives like the one I was threatened with. To appreciate why this is the case, we must understand who they benefit.

Although the HJS and similar think tanks like Policy Exchange and the Centre for Social Cohesion (CSC) call themselves 'independent' research bodies, it is unclear what exactly they are independent from. Their work is funded by vested interests, relies on militaristic colonial theories, and feeds into the heart of government.[4] For example, HJS produced much of the academic justification for Donald Trump's Muslim Ban.[5] They also conceived large elements of the theories that underpin the global counter-extremism industry. The official Prevent strategy document even cites CSC five times (CSC was absorbed into HJS in 2011).[6]

---

2   https://linkedin.com/pulse/brendan-simms-racist-corrupt-henry-jackson-society-matthew (accessed March 2021).

3   https://medium.com/insurge-intelligence/the-american-far-right-s-trojan-horse-in-westminster-6799f442d6ce (accessed March 2021).

4   Tom Griffin, David Miller and Tom Mills, 'The Neoconservative Movement: Think Tanks as Elite Elements of Social Movements from Above' in ed. Narzanin Massoumi, Tom Mills and David Miller, *What is Islamophobia? Racism, Social Movements and the state* (London: Pluto, 2017), p. 220.

5   https://bylinetimes.com/2020/10/26/trumpocracy-in-the-uk-government-links-with-steve-bannon-and-the-mercers/ (accessed March 2021).

6   Griffin, Miller and Mills, 'The Neoconservative Movement', pp. 224–5.

With such direct political influence, it is important to ask who such think tanks are funded by. Although HJS's donors are mostly undisclosed, investigations found that they tend to be of those who also donate tens of thousands to the US Republican Party and the UK Conservative Party, as well as other neoconservative and Islamophobic organisations like the David Horowitz Freedom Centre in the US.[7] Scholar, Sarah Marusek, found that the 14 think tanks most involved in spreading Islamophobic narratives globally – including HJS – are funded by the same 60 US-based family foundations and charities.[8] This means a tiny handful of a global capitalist class finance the ideas that underpin national and international policies. This undermines any 'democratic governance' that Britain, or other Western states claim. In fact, they would likely call such a situation elsewhere an oligarchy.

Moreover, Marusek's investigation also found that 75% of the 60 top funders of Islamophobic think tanks gave almost $169m to 'organisations identified as supporting Israel's occupation and/or settlements' between 2009–13.[9] Such settlements have been declared illegal by global bodies like the International Court of Justice and the UN. So the fact that HJS's funders are also major contributors to the illegal occupation of Palestine tells us that HJS's production of Islamophobic narratives are understood to play an important role in justifying real-world projects like settler colonialism. Indeed, Islamophobic theories and caricatures are often used to depoliticise Palestinian resistance to colonial occupation as simply irrational Muslim terrorism.

---

7   https://bylinetimes.com/2020/11/03/trumpocracy-in-the-uk-boris-johnsons-lobby-group-us-dark-money/ (accessed March 2021).

8   Sarah Marusek, 'The Transatlantic Network: Funding Islamophobia and Israeli Settlements' in ed. Massoumi et al, *What is Islamophobia* (London: Pluto Press, 2017).

9   Ibid., p. 200.

The business of security

It is not only think tanks and their funders who benefit from production of Islamophobic narratives, though. As explored throughout this book, private security and military corporations have profited astronomically due to theories about terrorism, extremism and security that increase demand for drone technologies, border surveillance or weapons for militarised policing and repressing dissent.

As a result, think tanks are just part of a multitude of bodies paid to generate knowledge that bends public and political opinion towards securitisation. For example, in the UK, the Government Communications Headquarters (GCHQ) – an intelligence operation – and the National Cyber Security Centre, fund PhDs and academic researchers to produce bodies of knowledge that justify expansion of their work. Another example is the International Centre for the Study of Radicalisation at King's College, University of London that exists to provide research explicitly for governance on terrorism and security. Therefore, as happened in colonial times, research funded by stakeholders invents a body of knowledge to their own interests. Think tanks are simply one location of this, and some scholars even describe a 'revolving door between policy think tanks like HJS' and those working in counter-extremism.[10]

These connections demonstrate that 'the power of the capitalist class depends also on its ability to control the state' and 'the state is the key element in maintaining the dominance of the capitalist class'.[11] Therefore, although we are told that the state 'rolls back' under neoliberalism, while it may well abandon

---

10   https://cage.ngo/imperialists-like-the-hjs-are-dangerously-out-of-touch-with-reality-its-time-to-call-them-out (accessed February 2021).

11   Norman Fairclough, *Language and Power* (London: Routledge, 2015).

marginalised people, it works hard to intervene on behalf of capitalist corporations. For instance, when HJS ran the 'Homeland Security' All-Party Parliamentary Group in Parliament between 2009–14, its advisory members included the former head of US Homeland Security, who was Chairman of BAE Systems at the time (2012–15).[12] BAE Systems is one of the world's biggest arms manufacturers with its top three markets being the US Department of Defence, India and Saudi Arabia. All three are engaged in brutal violence against their own citizens and foreign occupations and war – Saudi Arabia even use BAE fighter jets to murder Yemeni civilians in a war the British government claim to 'condemn' despite welcoming BAE's Chairman into the halls of Parliament for policymaking discussions led by a militaristic think tank.

Clearly, the research HJS produce bolsters securitisation and militarisation to the benefit of its funders, and such research also builds its own reputation for creating such narratives. This leads governments in countries such as the UK to commission it for their own Islamophobic policies. The Home Office gave HJS £83,452.32 between 2015–17 to produce a report about 'Islamist terrorism'.[13] All of this benefits the security industry which profit by subsequently selling states the tools of terror that research suggests they need. This cyclic set of relationships constitute a 'security-industrial-complex' (SIC). There can be no justice in our societies, and no semblance of peace, while such corporations, vested interests and their accompanying research bodies exist.

---

12   Tobias Ellwood and Mark Phillips, *Improving Efficiency, Interoperability and Resilience of our Blue Light Services* (London: APPG on Homeland Security, 2013).
13   https://opendemocracy.net/en/opendemocracyuk/revealed-uk-home-office-paid-80000-to-a-lobby-group-which-has-funded-conservative-mps/ (accessed January 2021).

News media

What is the role of the media in upholding the security-industrial-complex? Most newspapers in the UK are companies run for the profit of their billionaire owners. For instance, the *Times* is owned entirely by News Corporation, Rupert Murdoch's private business. In fact, Murdoch owns 70% of the UK's newspapers including the *Sun*, the *Times*, the *Sunday Times*, the *Press Association* and *Times Literary Supplement*. Of the other 30% of newspapers, the *Daily Mail* is privately owned by Viscount Rothermere, the *Telegraph* by the Barclays brothers, and the *Express* by Richard Desmond. These are not democratic organisations we can expect to provide rigorous journalism or hold to ethical standards. Their role is profit-making and opinion-formation. In Charles Umney's words, 'capital exerts disproportionate influence over what people think and what ideas are acceptable in capitalist societies, and it can do this for a fairly straightforward reason. Because, just as it controls the means of (commodity) production, it also controls the "means of mental production"'.[14] It is subsequently unsurprising that most newspapers do not run stories that scrutinise capitalism, imperialism or structures of racism that benefit them – or, as in the case I witnessed, that they are happy to collaborate with private interest groups like HJS.

Although TV and films portray journalism as an industry brimming with investigative work, the reality is often much duller. On top of making news stories out of private think tank's concerns, one of the key features of mainstream news today is generating stories based on what is trending online, as that is

---

14   Charles Umney, *Class Matters: Inequality and Exploitation in 21st Century Britain* (London: Pluto, 2018), p. 154.

likely to get more sales and clicks.[15] As journalist, Faima Bakkar, told me, 'the association of Islam with terror . . . has become a bit of a cash cow for the media. People are going to click on these types of stories, or buy them in print, because it aligns with their preconceived notions of Muslims', or because it's so controversial. 'If people consume this content in their droves, it sends media heads the message that there is vast interest in these types of stories. So, of course, they will continue circulating them . . . and people who share these stories to criticise them also end up popularising them which doesn't exactly motivate editors to stop publishing such content.' This means journalists who could be scrutinising the dangerous monopoly of power in the hands of a global capitalist class or the violent expansion of the SIC, instead spout Islamophobia that benefits those very same interests.

Many conversations about tackling Islamophobia in the media miss this structural dynamic. Instead, they revolve around representation, suggesting that better representation of Muslims is the antidote to racism. But this assumes Islamophobia is the result of inaccuracy or negativity, not the result of the very framing and premise of news stories, the questions considered, and the contexts ignored. There are some who therefore file complaints about media inaccuracies with IPSO – the Independent Press Standards Organisation. But since IPSO only take account of 'factual' inaccuracies, and newspapers print their 'corrections' in small print on an inside page weeks after the story has already made an impact, we are left with the question of how to seek serious accountability for systemic Islamophobia.[16]

---

15   Nathan Lean, *The Islamophobia Industry: How the right manufactures hatred of Muslims* (London: Pluto, 2017), p. 88.
16   Hacked Off, Hate, White supremacism, the press and the absence of regulation 2017–2020, (London: Hacked Off, 2020).

For instance, in 2017 the *Times* published a series of front-page spreads, the most notorious stating, 'Christian child forced into Muslim foster care'. Tower Hamlets council, where the foster case took place, raised a complaint with IPSO because almost every detail in the story was incorrect. Their complaint was accepted so the *Times* printed a tiny correction inside their paper. By that time, though, the original false story had thousands of racist comments on it and had been circulated and re-published in white supremacist forums where it was treated as fact and generated further commentary. Since then, a court ruling found the entire premise of the story to be untrue, but no rectification has, or arguably can, be made.[17]

This story shows us the limits of seeking justice through the news media itself. IPSO is funded by its member publishers and its board members have careers in print journalism. They do not have a standard of journalistic ethics but seek to make sure the 'Editor's Code' – written by those inside the industry – is followed. As Faima told me, 'although publications take IPSO seriously . . . certain publications may risk running an inaccurate story, because at the end of the day, even with legal ramifications, they will have offset it with the amount of views they get, or prints they sell – they might even win new viewers and followers.' Therefore, as many small-print corrections as may be printed, they cannot dent the Islamophobic corporate machine whose goal is not to get stories right, but to serve their capitalist owners financially, and ideologically.

Moreover, better representation of Muslims can also be absorbed into this system. In Chapter 6 we saw *Vogue*'s coverage of Muslim women in the counter-extremism industry. That

17   https://newstatesman.com/politics/media/2018/09/the-times-muslim-christian-child-foster-care-tower-hamlets-court-ruling-ipso   (accessed   February 2021).

coverage did not depict women 'negatively', but it promoted the SIC which polices, punishes and harms Muslim women around the world, every day. Better representation is not a good in of itself, then. It can be co-opted to advance nationalist, imperialist and neoliberal narratives. For instance, coverage celebrating the lives of Muslim doctors who died from COVID-19 was markedly different from 'terrorist' imagery, but even in its sympathy it implied that the only Muslim lives that can be valued are those that die in servitude to the nation; not undocumented and incarcerated Muslims, or the ones killed in Britain's imperialist wars.

We need to move our demands beyond mainstream media representation. News media cannot bring us justice unless it actively and critically investigates and reveals state and structural violence – which it cannot do as long as it is run for the profit of those who benefit from such violence.

Regurgitating Islamophobia

In his book *The Islamophobia Industry*, Nathan Lean shows that another reason news coverage is so frequently Islamophobic is due to far-right cult figures creating moral panics about Muslims on social media.[18] Their sensationalist posts, videos and other commentary are often republished across social media where they are picked up by mainstream media outlets. Lean focuses on Pamela Geller and Richard Spencer in the US, but in the UK we might think of Britain First's Paul Golding, the English Defence League's former leader, Tommy Robinson, Katie Hopkins or Carl Benjamin. Their volumes of videos and posts

18   Lean, *Islamophobia Industry*.

are sometimes covered by news outlets simply due to the controversy they create.

For instance, in 2017, after the Manchester arena bombing, Katie Hopkins tweeted, 'we need a final solution' in a longer Islamophobic tirade. The tweet was quickly deleted but screenshotted, reposted and picked up by media outlets.[19] Although most coverage condemned her, by making her tweet their basis, her 'final solution' narrative was given credence as a topic of discussion. Such attention from followers and adversaries has enabled Hopkins to have a number of newspaper columns over the years and to be invited onto mainstream platforms to debate her views. As a columnist at the Mail Online she fabricated a story about a British Muslim family being prevented from visiting Disneyland by US authorities because they had links to al-Qaeda.[20] By the time she had to issue an apology, the story had a life of its own.

Despite pitching themselves as besieged members of communities harmed by Muslims, people like Hopkins and Robinson are far from counter-hegemonic grassroots figures. They make lucrative careers from Islamophobia. Lots of their funding comes from private American donors, and oftentimes from the very same donors who fund Islamophobic think tanks, or the think tanks themselves.[21] While think tanks produce the 'academic' rationale for Islamophobia, these cult-figures stoke Islamophobia among a wider public. Even when they are condemned, they get to shape the narrative that benefits the SIC, and they are paid to do so.

---

19   https://theguardian.com/uk-news/2017/may/23/manchester-attack-police-investigate-katie-hopkins-final-solution-tweet (accessed December 2020).
20   https://theguardian.com/media/2016/dec/19/mail-pays-out-150k-to-muslim-family-over-katie-hopkins-column (accessed February 2020).
21   Lean, *Islamophobia Industry*.

Profiting from persecution

In 2011, Anders Breivik murdered 77 people in Norway by detonating a bomb that killed eight and by individually shooting 69 others at a Labour Party youth camp. On the morning of the attacks he distributed a manifesto describing his motivations. It was mainly a collation of other people's writings – Richard Spencer's work was cited 162 times, and Breivik praised Pamela Geller's blog. When people pointed out that Breivik took their rhetoric to its logical conclusion of massacre, Geller responded that he 'was targeting future leaders of the party responsible for flooding Norway with Muslims who refuse to assimilate, who commit major violence against Norwegian natives, including violent gang rapes, with impunity, and who live on the dole'.

Despite this justification of mass murder, *Times* coverage of Pamela Geller has only ever referred to her as an 'activist' and 'campaigner'; they do not deem her an apologist for terrorism. It is worth considering who is and is not considered an apologist for terrorism in light of the email I received from the *Times* myself. Their concerns about me surrounded 'affiliation' to CAGE, an organisation they described as 'accused in the past of being apologists for terrorists'. This refers to a press conference CAGE called about Muhammed Emwazi when he was found to be the ISIS executioner 'Jihadi John' in 2015. In the past, prior to being charged for any terrorism-related offense, Emwazi had been in touch with CAGE about harassment he was experiencing from UK security services – including attempts to recruit him as an informant. The press conference CAGE called was to share this evidence as important context for the conversation around Emwazi. In the conference CAGE's Director of Research, Asim Qureshi, recalled Emwazi had been 'extremely gentle' when he first contacted the organisation, highlighting that significant events must have contributed to his transformation into 'Jihadi John'.

However, right-wing press latched onto and decontextualised this comment, reporting that CAGE 'said killer was a "beautiful man"'.[22] Instead of addressing the evidence about the intelligence services role in Emwazi's life, the narrative that came out of the conference was of CAGE being terrorist-apologists. The slur was easy to stick to a Muslim-led organisation working for the rights of those affected by War on Terror legislation. It was used to delegitimise their work in mainstream circles where the threat of being seen to support CAGE became a coercive tool that led some to stop their affiliations, and even pushed several financial backers to walk away.

The fact that the HJS and the *Times* attempted to use this smear to discredit me as a Radio 4 documentary presenter demonstrates how desperately important voices that hold the state to account are. CAGE has become a stick to beat any Muslim who dares speak of the violence of the state's national security system or the War on Terror in the UK. Dozens of activists have had smear pieces of this kind published about them, or threatened, as in my case. This is because, as this chapter has shown, there are powerful financial stakeholders invested in producing Islamophobic narratives that bolster imperialism, militarism and securitisation, and they are also invested in eradicating all narratives that oppose them.

But the fact that global corporate networks worth billions feel the need to pursue individual grassroot voices one by one, ironically shows that our voices are more threatening than we even know. We threaten to expose a system they have meticulously crafted to their advantage. A system where private financial

---

22 https://www.opendemocracy.net/en/opendemocracyuk/apologists-for-terror-or-defenders-of-human-righ/ (accessed March 2021).

interests fund organisations to produce 'evidence' that profits their security corporations and colonial and military ventures; and that regurgitates Islamophobic narratives in academic spaces, mainstream news media and the internet, to manufacture consent for its genocidal project. We cannot simply 'push back' against this system in hopes of more participation or representation. We must uproot it. This is both an ideological and material project; we must shred apart the narratives that uphold this system, as well as the system itself.

Conclusion: A safe world on our own terms

Say, I seek refuge with the Lord of the daybreak. – Quran 113:1

I for one believe that if you give people a thorough under-standing of what confronts them and the basic causes that produce it, they'll create their own program, and when the people create a program, you get action.'[1] – Malcolm X

Islamophobia is not and was never about Muslims. By claiming to be, it has invented the phantom of 'the Muslim threat' that is mobilised to justify and hide a web of international, national and border violence in the name of security. While this has secured states and capital against dissent, critique, accountability and redistribution; the marginalised, racialised and dispossessed of the world have become *less safe*. We are bombed, occupied, caged, policed, deported, disabled, displaced, tortured, moni-tored and killed in the name of security. But Islamophobia is not a 'new racism', nor has it existed since time immemorial. And far from being a force that is external to and damaging the normal working of the system, Islamophobia is a sign of European colonial violence, liberal race-making and white supremacy's secularism, persisting.

---

1 https://teachingamericanhistory.org/library/document/at-the-audubon/ (accessed July 2021).

The War on Terror does not show us that international legal norms have been disregarded; it shows us the continuation of colonial projects of resource extraction. National security policies do not threaten healthy liberal democracy, such democracy was always a veneer for coercively policing racialised and exploited people. Counter-extremism surveillance has not uniquely undermined freedom of speech, speech has only ever been free when non-threatening to the hegemony of racism and capitalism. And secularism has not failed, it was always a part of white supremacy's racial classification system. Therefore, calls for positive representation, more hate-crime legislation and unconscious-bias training have been misguided. If we are serious about ending Islamophobia, our demands must address its root causes.

In Sivanandan's words,

> In fighting our specific causes we need also to be aware of the common cause they spring from and address ourselves to both at once – and so forge the alliances we need to win the battle. For globalisation is a complete system and unravelling one strand of it at a time does not unravel the whole. Single issue struggles may usher in piecemeal reform but not radical change.[2]

Therefore, by focusing on *uprooting*, not just 'lessening' Islamophobia, we move towards this deeper change.

A structural analysis of Islamophobia helps us to see that as long as the Left is wedded to the need for national security policies or concedes to anti-immigrant rhetoric that divides workers, it is not pro-labour or anti-capitalist. Rather, it upholds

---

2   https://irr.org.uk/article/racism-liberty-and-the-war-on-terror/ (accessed January 2021).

logics that states and capital use to repress and exploit the world's mostly racialised and dispossessed working-class. Likewise, for as long as struggles against gendered and sexual violence seek to give the state more policing powers and impose a secular understanding of 'freedom' onto women, they are not resisting patriarchy, but colluding with it to make marginalised women more vulnerable. This analysis also makes it clear that Islamophobia can only be ended if the white supremacy that sharply upholds anti-Black racism is absolutely demolished. That means Black Lives Matter and every other struggle to abolish white supremacy and racial hierarchy are central to uprooting Islamophobia. Until non-Black Muslims actively respond to this, we will continue to uphold Islamophobia, too.

'Green Deals' and climate change activism that imagine national change as their horizon fail to identify Islamophobic imperialism and racial capitalism as leading causes of ecological catastrophe. This means they are invested in the continued exclusion of people displaced by the environmental impact of Western economic development. Islamophobia can only end if such people are able to live and move free from the violence of borders and not be displaced by capitalism and its climate catastrophes in the first place. Thus, uprooting Islamophobia demands resisting every imperialist dynamic from war, to trade, to the work of the World Bank, and transnational corporations. As well as aiding those resisting state repression across the world, including in so-called 'Muslim' states.

It can feel daunting to face the need to re-imagine the world, but, as I hope this book has demonstrated, that is our only choice. And, as Kaba states, it means 'there are many places to start, infinite opportunities to collaborate and endless imaginative interventions and experiments . . . The question is not "what do we have now and how can we make it better?" but, "what can we imagine for ourselves and the world?"[3]

In the immediate term, something every one of us can do to imagine another world is to change the language we use. If everyone who reads this book commits to stop using the word 'terrorism' to describe non-state actors' violence, and the word 'security' to describe state violence, we can collectively raise consciousness about the root causes of violence that lie in the histories and structures around us, not marginalised people's cultures, ideas, languages or religions. We must be unashamed to name the origins of violence as colonialism's white supremacy, secularism and capitalism, not simply to 'be woke', but with deep understanding of its truth. There is a place for everyone in this work.

We can also forge a broader collective consensus that the state and policing do not keep us safe. Critically analysing Islamophobia helps us see that prisons, police and punitive systems solve neither violence nor social injustice; they are tools of oppression. From counterterror policing that terrorises Muslims, to border enforcement that brutalises migrants and undocumented people, to 'ordinary' policing that makes life unliveable for racialised, disabled, poor and especially Black people. This means we must demand the repeal of all counterterror laws and topple their accompanying profit-hungry security industrial complex. We must expose the SIAC 'secret evidence' system to demand its abolition; and refuse to comply with the regulation of immigrants and refugees. We must resist the state's attempt to make us reliant on counter-extremism funding through finding ways to collectively support our communities without accepting to criminalise each other. And everybody bound to the Prevent

---

3   Mariame Kaba, *We Do This 'til We Free Us: Abolitionist Organizing and Transforming Justice*, (Chicago: Haymarket Books, 2021), p. 5.

duty must refuse the obligation to criminalise those we have been conditioned to view as suspicious, and instead be mindful of the *causes* of vulnerability in people around them.

But we must also expand such demands and endeavours to include resisting all pre-emptive and other forms of policing. Calls to 'abolish' policing systems that do not address all forms of policing are unproductive. Yet many conversations around abolition have overlooked counterterrorism, which not only risks leaving the wider policing apparatus intact, it risks not taking heed of Muslims' experiences of Prevent, counter-extremism and integration work. Those experiences demonstrate that replacing policing with 'community alternatives' is not a solution, but often a way that policing persists. Instead of seeking these alternatives, let us ask what conditions would be required for us to be safe from harm, exploitation and injustice in the first place. Let us assert that we, not terrorising states, or a security industrial complex, have better means of ending violence – and they begin with ending state and capitalist violence and therefore landing at another justice system altogether.

Therefore, let us demand full public investment into health, education, housing and well-being resources that can better deal with the problems policing claims to address. Within this vision we can also seek to replace immigration detention, deportations, militarism and the security and arms trades with safe legal routes, statuses and housing to people seeking asylum; and an end to the imperialist wars, debt bondage of the Global South, and capitalist relations that cause climate change, displacement and underpin the degradation and misery of most everything else. Islamophobia can only be eradicated by uprooting the world as we know it.

This should be a reminder to any who are still unclear that the solution to Islamophobia is not to have more Muslims wielding tools of state violence in government, or corporate capitalist power. We cannot resolve Islamophobia by owning more businesses or accumulating profit as is sometimes imagined. Replicating capitalism while hoping to be the capitalists, will not free us. Nor will patriotism, proving we 'really are British', 'good citizens' or 'not all terrorists'. There is a famous Islamic narration that the Prophet Muhammad ﷺ said, 'Whosoever of you sees an evil, let him change it with his hand; and if he is not able to do so, then [let him change it] with his tongue; and if he is not able to do so, then with his heart – and that is the weakest of faith.'[4] May we strive to be of those who act, and if not, then at least detest our complicity in the violence this book has identified.

Untangling ourselves from complicity is not an overnight process, however; it is the work of life. If we want to build a just world, we must confront the ways that we make each other unsafe and ask our deepest selves about whose oppression we choose to ignore in our imagining of the future. As Robin D. G. Kelley reminds us, 'making a revolution is not a series of clever manoeuvres and tactics but a process that can and must transform us.'[5] Are we willing to move from a mode of 'solidarity' and 'activism' that is performative and aims to raise our own social capital, to one that is difficult, often unnoticeable and profoundly changing? In the Quran it is stated, 'Indeed, Allah will not change the condition of a people until they change what is in themselves.'[6] It is for this reason that I do not end this book with blueprint answers. The ways we change this world-system

---

4   https://sunnah.com/nawawi40:34 (accessed March 2021).

5   Robin D. G. Kelley, Freedom Dreams: The Black Radical Imagination, (Boston: Beacon Press, 2002), p. 12.

6   Quran, 13:11.

involve changing our deepest desires for praise, recognition and status that have haunted me even in writing this work.

I have tried to write primarily to demonstrate that this world-order is not accidental. It had a beginning, and it has beneficiaries, therefore, it can be ended, uprooted and upturned. Indeed, the only knowledge I hold as absolute truth is that there is no earthly authority that cannot be upturned. The Zapatistas, a revolutionary indigenous people who seek liberation from the Mexican state, refer to this world-system as 'larga noche de los quinientos años': the long night of 500 years, that has robbed them of humanity and autonomy.[7] A night of 500 years cannot be expected to come to an end in five years, or even 50. Perhaps it is not within our generational power to draw the day out of a night so long. But it is within our power to struggle, demand, believe in and pray for it so that someday, even if we do not live to see it, others may witness a daybreak.

---

7   https://palabra.ezln.org.mx/comunicados/1996/1996_01_01_a.htm (accessed July 2021).

Thanks to our Patreon subscriber:

Ciaran Kane

Who has shown generosity and
comradeship in support of our publishing.

Check out the other perks you get by subscribing
to our Patreon – visit patreon.com/plutopress.

Subscriptions start from £3 a month.